Mental handicap

Mental handicap
Social science perspectives

Edited by
Steve Baldwin
and
John Hattersley

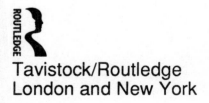
Tavistock/Routledge
London and New York

First published in 1991
by Routledge
11 New Fetter Lane, London EC4P 4EE

Simultaneously published in the USA and Canada
by Routledge
a division of Routledge, Chapman and Hall Inc.
29 West 35th Street, New York, NY 10001

Wordprocessed on to disk by Amy Boyle
Laserprinted by LaserScript Limited, Mitcham, Surrey

Printed and bound in Great Britain by
Mackays of Chatham PLC, Chatham, Kent

British Library Cataloguing in Publication Data

Mental handicap: Social science perspectives.
    1. Social services for mentally handicapped persons
    I. Baldwin, Steve, 1957– II. Hattersley, John 362.38

Library of Congress Cataloging in Publication Data

Mental handicap: social science perspectives/edited by
    Steve Baldwin and John Hattersley.
    p. cm.
    Includes bibliographical references
    1. Mentally handicapped. 2. Mentally handicapped – Services for.
    I. Baldwin, Steve, 1957–. II. Hattersley, John.
    HV3004.M367 1990   90-10798
    362.3'8-dc20   CIP

ISBN 0-415-00596-5

Contents

Tables and figures

Tables

Figures

Contributors

Andy Alaszewski is Head of the Department of Social Policy and Professional Studies at the University of Hull. He has published widely, including three books in mental handicap, with a particular focus on evaluating the development of services for people with learning difficulties. He has been involved in research on the development of policies and services for people with a mental handicap since 1972.

Steve Baldwin is Consultant Psychologist at Neighbourhood Networks Project, TACADE, Salford; he is also Visiting Research Fellow at Polytechnic Southwest, Plymouth. He was previously Research Fellow at the Department of Psychiatry, University of Dundee. Steve has worked in substance abuse; gerontology, learning difficulties and forensic services. He is specifically interested in neighbourhood evaluations.

Michael Bayley is a freelance writer and researcher. He was formerly Lecturer in the Department of Sociological Studies, University of Sheffield. As well as publishing extensively in the field of learning difficulties, he was specifically involved in the initiation and development of the Dinnington Project. This innovative neighbourhood work has considerable implications for how services might develop for people with learning difficulties.

Roger Blunden is Programme Director at the King's Fund Centre in London. He was previously Director of the Applied Mental Handicap Research Unit in Cardiff. Roger has published extensively in the field of learning difficulties, both with regard to specific local projects, and about the Welsh NIMROD evaluation. At present, he is involved in service development with innovative services in various parts of Britain.

John Hattersley is General Manager in Mental Health Services Sheffield. He was previously Unit General Manager and Head of Speciality, Mental Handicap Services, Sheffield. John has published widely in the area of applied behaviour analysis, and service provision, and is a member of the Development Team. He has developed four Departments of Psychology, and impacted on the national template of services for people with learning difficulties.

Alan Haycox is a Regional Health Economist at Northwest Regional Health Authority in Manchester. Previously he has completed local projects in learning difficulties services in Kent and Yorkshire. As an economist, he is particularly interested in cost-effectiveness and cost efficiency questions about de-institutionalisation and its impact on people with learning difficulties.

Martin Jackaman is a Senior Social Worker in Nottingham. He has extensive practical experience in the provision of services to people with learning difficulties. As a member of a service provision team, he has developed a particular interest in the relationship between clients, their parents, and other family members.

Ian Macdonald is Director of the Mental Handicap Services Unit, BIOSS. He has published extensively in the field of learning difficulties, in particular in the areas of personal assessment, values and ideology. As well as providing a national teaching and training function for specialist workers, the Unit provides an advisory input to central government. In addition to his role as Director, Ian also works as a Personnel/Selection Consultant in Australasia, and in project work with ethnic populations.

Bie Nio Ong is a Lecturer in the Centre for Health Planning and Management at the University of Keele. She is engaged in putting research into practice by involving consultancy and training in NHS management. As a sociological commentator, she is specifically interested in themes of feminism and sexism, and their influence in the field of handicap and disability.

Tim Robinson is Lecturer in Social Work at the University of Sheffield. His previously published work reflects an interest in the relationships between professionals and clients. He is also the parent of a disabled child and has recently been involved in running a respite care scheme.

Ken Wright is Head of Department at the Social Policy Research Unit at the University of York. He has published widely in the area of cost-effectiveness of alternative, non-institutionalised services for people with learning difficulties. He is involved with local and regional projects in Yorkshire and the North East, with a specific focus on quality of care/quality of life themes.

Acknowledgements

The Editors would like to thank Gail Hammond and May MacPhail for their invaluable work in the preparation of this typescript. Thanks are due to Ken Barton and Carfax for permission to include chapter nine, previously published in Disability Handicap and Society.

Some of this work was completed during receipt of project funding from the Alcohol Education and Research Council and Charity Projects, to whom warm thanks are extended.

Special thanks to Lynda Goldman for her advice and assistance during the completion of this text.

Chapter one

The future of normalisation

John Hattersley

Normalisation has become a widely used term and is based upon a wide range of literature (Flynn and Nitsch, 1980). The definition of normalisation has not remained static and it may be helpful to trace its history. Bank-Mikkelsen (1969) proposed that 'mentally retarded' people should be allowed to 'obtain an existence as close to normal as possible'. This view had an impact on services in Denmark in that the Danish Mental Retardation Act (1985) had included the statement 'to create an existence for the mentally retarded, as close to normal as possible'. This seemed to imply that someone would set up, on behalf of the person labelled 'mentally retarded', an environment which mimicked, as far as possible, normal living. Within this environment the person was expected to exist. This interpretation may do some injustice to the original intention of the writer but there is a strong feeling that the 'mentally retarded' person is not expected to be an active participant in the process.

Nirje (1973), from experiences in Sweden, defined normalisation as 'making available to the mentally retarded patterns and conditions of everyday life which are as close as possible to the norms and patterns of the mainstream of society'. Once again these ideas were incorporated into the statutes of the country in an unsystematic way. The implication was still that the 'mentally retarded' person passively received services, rather than being an active agent in the process. There is room for some confusion about the interpretation of this definition; it is unclear whether 'patterns and conditions of everyday life' referred to an end state or to the means by which that state was to be achieved (or both).

In the United States of America normalisation was redefined as 'the utilization of means which are as culturally normative as possible' (Wolfensberger, 1972) and was used in relation to services for a range

1

of clients, including people with a mental handicap. The limitation of this definition was again that it was not clear whether it referred to both means and ends. Much of the subsequent confusion in the related literature, highlighted by Wolfensberger, might be traced to this poor conceptual clarity. This limitation was acknowledged in the literature, and as a consequence the definition was extended. The principle of normalisation was stated to be 'the use of culturally normative means (familiar, valued techniques, tools, methods) in order to *enable* a person's life conditions (income, housing, health services, etc.), appearance (clothes, grooming, etc.), experiences (adjustment, feelings, etc.), and status and reputation labels (attitudes of others etc.)'.

Two other definitions of the principle of normalisation have been offered. In 1982 it was proposed that normalisation meant 'as much as possible the use of culturally valued means to enable/establish and/or maintain valued social roles for people'. In this definition the importance of values, as a basis for the principle had become much clearer. These values, placed within the context of a particular culture, increased the probability that the principle would change with time and place. This idea was supported by the recent suggestion that the term 'normalisation' be discarded and replaced by 'social role valorization' (Wolfensberger, 1983). The proposed change was based on the view that 'the highest goals of the principle of normalisation have recently been clarified to the establishment, enhancement, or defense of the social role(s) of a person or group, via the enhancement of people's social images and personal competencies'. Wolfensberger has defended his use of the word 'valorization', whilst acknowledging that the dictionary definition gives it the meaning of 'attempting to give market value or price to a commodity'. He was concerned that this might give the impression that people with a mental handicap could be viewed as a commodity. He estimated, however, that in practice people knew the word and predicted that there was not a 'compelling negative image juxtaposition'. He argued that its use should be reserved to refer to the value that is placed by society on the role of people and not the value that is placed on the people themselves.

This proposal met a mixed response from a critical audience which had become increasingly polarised in its reaction to the normalisation debate. In addition there was a risk that the focus of the debate had become an argument about semantics, rather than a way of helping people to improve human services.

Wolfensberger has always recognised that the practice of devaluing people in a society is 'culturally relative'. He suggested two primary goals to be achieved in overcoming the problem. First, it was necessary to reduce or prevent the occurrence of those physical or behavioural features of a person which might lead others to devalue that person. Second, a change in the values and perceptions of society was required so that any feature which might in the past have encouraged society to devalue the person no longer had this effect. To achieve these ends, two methods were proposed. An individual's skills or 'competencies' should be improved and broadened, to be more like those found in the non-handicapped population; the value of an individual as perceived by society should be enhanced so as to obtain 'maximal feasible acceptance of individual differences'. On close examination the 'theory' and practice of normalisation may turn out to be far less radical than they first appear. Many proponents of the theory recognise that the best opportunity for change in the way devalued groups are treated by society lies in using the current 'strengths' of society and helping devalued people to fit into that society. This might be a sensible strategy for change but it assumes that the values and norms of behaviour and appearance in society are worth striving after. There are many examples throughout history where individuals have struggled to become acceptable to a particular group by imitating the group's values and norms, only to have those same values and norms exposed as worthless, dangerous or evil by other, more discerning, people.

In attempting to clarify his position on these matters, Wolfensberger has argued that one of the most common misconceptions about the principle of normalisation is 'that it implies that each person should be fitted to the statistical norm of the society'. He points out that there are three factors in a society which contribute to the degree of normalisation that is judged to be achieved by any measure. First, there are the cultural values, which may be viewed as an ideal set of standards against which people can be measured, and which are rarely achieved by any individual. Second, there are the cultural norms, which prescribe those behaviours or appearances that are generally expected in particular situations. And finally, there are the statistical norms of behaviour or appearances which actually occur in society. Wolfensberger postulated that a measure becomes more 'normalising' the closer it is to the ideal set of cultural values.

This approach does not appear to encourage and [might] discourage even any questioning of the status quo. Society's values are left untouched, while the responsibility for any change in the direction of

3

those values is placed on the disabled and devalued person. There are many features of any culture that are relatively static and determine a consistent pattern of behaviour in most people. Much of what every member of society is encouraged and expected to learn is based upon a set of social mores and regular behaviour patterns.

Normalisation, as portrayed in the literature, appears not to challenge these dominant values, and, by definition, appears to endorse them. Before imposing such values on people with a mental handicap, it should be possible to investigate whether there are other values which might be used to help set more realistic goals for them. If alternative values are to be chosen, it will be important to try to avoid placing already vulnerable people at the leading edge of any movement for change in society, where they could attract more attention which, in the short term, could lead to further devaluation. With the right support, on the other hand, such individuals could become highly valued for their part in a process of change which is likely to be increasingly valued by society.

On closer examination the values encountered in the normalisation literature appear to be based on a western culture, in particular that of North America. Commentators have suggested that such values include capitalism, materialism, competitiveness, individualism, and achievement or success within a nuclear family (Ni Ong, 1983).

Integration is dependent on an acceptance of the society and its values into which individuals are to be integrated. A primary focus in integration is to help people move from institutional residential care into ordinary houses in a local neighbourhood. This appears to match the vigorous movement for 'care in the community', which is a central theme of the British Government's policy for mental handicap services. Underlying this theme is a set of values which includes a belief in the nuclear family as an ideal way of providing care. The family is viewed as a secure environment in which the father provides the money, which enables material needs to be met, while the mother provides the care, particularly for the dependent members of the family. Such values have led many women themselves to become totally dependent upon their husbands, in a society where independence is achieved through the medium of personal wealth. The long, hard hours of care undertaken by women in families is assumed to be done out of love and not require genuine recompense. In short, these values lead to the exploitation of many women. If the normalisation movement intends to support such values it would be helpful to have a clear statement to this effect. With their explicit focus on values and their impact on people with a mental handicap, proponents of normalisation should accept responsibility for making explicit the values of the society into which devalued people are to be integrated, and for questioning whether such values are acceptable.

The stress placed by Wolfensberger and others on enhancing the 'personal competencies' and valued social role has a logical corollary: the need for improved methods of teaching the necessary skills. A natural contender for the supply of an effective technology of teaching is behaviour analysis. Behavioural technology has been declared a value-free methodology for achieving behaviour change in individuals, groups and systems. For example, Gambrill stated that 'the discovery of systematic relationships between behaviour and the environment does not inform us as to how this knowledge should be employed' (Gambrill, 1978). To illustrate, the fact that it is possible to set up a stimulus to have a clear controlling relationship with respect to a given behaviour says nothing about the social value of such a relationship. Neither does it place any particular value upon the stimulus or the behaviour themselves.

One mechanism (or 'dynamic') singled out by the normalisation proponents to be used in a positive way with devalued persons is that of imitation. It is easy to reflect upon the selective evolutionary processes that would have led to the survival of individuals and groups susceptible to learning through imitation and modelling. Although it is still poorly understood, this mechanism helps establish large complex repertoires in individuals without their needing to be exposed to the gradual shaping process that was probably required to bring about the first examples of such behaviours. But imitation is only one small part of the available knowledge about learning and teaching that should be made available to help people who have behavioural deficits. Much of this knowledge, however, may not be as value-free as it first appears.

The first step in setting up a teaching programme to improve the competencies of any individual is to assess their present level of skills. There are now many assessment instruments available, designed to help teachers and trainers to be more objective in their assessments and to provide a baseline against which progress can be measured. Such instruments are also used to help determine the focus for any intervention. Bercovici has pointed out that in many assessment instruments 'there seems to be an implicit "world-at-large" to which human beings are presumed to adapt .... This world-at-large is the world that those who devise and administer assessment instruments are most familiar with –

"the dominant culture"'(Bercovici, 1983). This can prevent the assessor from making an accurate interpretation of the observed behaviours which should, in practice, be judged against the setting and the sub-culture in which they have developed and occur. A close analysis of the functional relationships which exist between a behaviour and its setting is likely to reveal that, although the behaviour has a form which is far from normal when judged against the world-at-large, in that setting it is not only lawful or rational, but is very adaptive.

The assessment process often is based implicitly upon a medical or clinical model in which there is an assumption that the behaviours measured in the individual can be compared against a normative set of expected behaviours. Any differences detected in the individual's behaviour automatically leads to the conclusion that there is something wrong with that individual. In practice, the behaviours observed might be more accurately interpreted as 'normal' in that particular setting, if only the professional making the judgement could free herself from the culture-bound assessment process and her own culture-bound value system.

Normalisation has been proposed as a model which can (or should) be used as a universal principle upon which to organise human ser-vices. It has been stated that the Wolfensberger formulation is an overall conceptual model which can be used to govern the design and conduct of virtually any human service. No doubt there are many other frameworks, including Marxism, socialism and conservatism, which also claim their own universal principles to determine how all services should be organised.

The ecological (or green) perspective has gradually become a coherent statement of alternative social values which has implications for both the means and the ends of service delivery. Porritt has expressed the view that western industrial societies have produced an ethos in which aggressive individualism, with competition as a key motivating force, is highly valued (Porritt, 1984). By definition, the 'success' of certain individuals, via competition, guarantees that other individuals must 'fail'. A society which values achievement will naturally value those persons who achieve. In such a society it is highly likely that less able individuals will never be truly valued. As an alternative, a much higher value could be placed upon co-operation and effort. This would enable people with disabilities to participate and become valued by society without being high achievers. In contrast, the normalisation emphasis on increasing the social value of individuals by enhancing the value of their social roles through enhancing 'personal competency' bows to society's present values, apparently without question. It places on the individual the responsibility to change and to compete in the social arena on the same terms as other people. The longer-term perspective may be better served by challenging the competitive values. The work ethic in modern industrial societies has placed an emphasis on the product and the profit that can be made. The 'wealth' generated by expanding industries has helped to finance the public services, but it has also produced a divided society, with a wealthy elite determining more and more of social values and government policy. At the same time this industrial economy, which emphasises expansion and the stimulation of demand to sustain that expansion, places greater and greater demands upon decreasing natural resources – resources which provide the energy and raw materials for the end-products, but which are generally not replaceable. As well as 'wealth-producing goods' there are additional, unwanted end-products: industrial waste and polluting side-effects.

In addition to these unwanted end-products, many of the carefully sought-after end-products, particularly the chemicals which play a growing part in everyone's life through their use in agriculture, medicine and industry, have the frightening potential to disturb the ecological balance and to poison, disable or kill. For years there has been an unquestioning acceptance of these products, many of which only now are demonstrating their toxic effects. Powerful industrialists justify the need for the end-products, stimulate demand, and carefully underplay the potential dangers, even opposing anti-pollution measures and laws, all in the name of producing more wealth. At the same time products such as pesticides, which may be banned in the country in which they are made, are sold to Third World countries, only to be returned to their country of origin incorporated in food imported from the Third World. The short-term profit motive is incompatible with long-term survival.

Within this ethos, there has been an imaginative movement to improve the integration and to 'valorize the role' of people with a mental handicap by helping them obtain paid employment (Wolfensberger, 1983). Many examples in the literature (Bellamy et al., 1979; Feinmann, 1987) have focused on the world of industry to supply the jobs required. Bellamy et al. make it clear from their perspective that 'the current trend towards vocational training with retarded individuals (sic) is based on three general value judgements or assumptions: the importance of

7

normalisation, a focus on deinstitutionalization and a belief in maximizing personal independence'. They argue that the objectives set for any individual in their programming should be congruent with the behaviour expected of 'normal, same-aged individuals'. Also, because adults in our society spend time working, and place great importance on that work, vocational competence is an important goal for people with a mental handicap.

The main body of their book is taken up with two themes: the behavioural methods designed to maximise each person's chances of learning; and an overriding emphasis on teaching those skills that will enable each person to become a productive link in a 'productive environment', based upon the current industrial society. Behavioural methods could be used to teach almost any skill, and do not require automatically to be linked to some industrial process. This is not to imply that a modern society can or should attempt to move away from the manufacture of necessary products. What is essential is to adjust our values towards 'finding and sustaining such means of creating wealth as will allow us to meet the genuine needs of all people without damaging our fragile biosphere. It implies a straight choice between what we have now (a consumer economy) and what we will need in the near future (a conserver economy) (Porritt, 1984). Before deciding on how to adjust our values, new questions should be answered, as: will this development harm the environment? Will the process consume scarce, non-renewable resources? Will it improve the general quality of life on this planet? Is the product and the process in the long-term interests of society and the workers? Is this another example of a small number of individuals obtaining short-term wealth, in present financial terms, at the expense of the long-term well-being of the planet?

All these questions could and should be asked about any new development. They could certainly be asked about any project designed to help people with a mental handicap develop work skills and obtain employment. It can be argued that it was the industrial society itself which played a significant part in the removal of people with a mental handicap and other socially devalued individuals from society as a whole. A radical review and adjustment of this value system could have many long-term positive effects for people presently devalued by society. Moves towards economic activity which is based on greater self-reliance at a local level, with an emphasis on meeting the primary needs of people through socially useful products, could be led by work projects designed to provide real employment for people who have a mental handicap.

In a society which includes several disadvantaged groups there is considerable competition for limited resources. Which group actually receives these resources is determined by many complex factors. In Britain, following a series of scandals highlighted by the media (for example, the enquiry at Ely Hospital), services for people with a mental handicap were given priority. Resource holders were encouraged to make more resources available to provide services to this client group. In particular the need to set up and recruit for a range of specialist posts was highlighted. Several professions, including community nursing, social work, occupational therapy, clinical psychology and physiotherapy all benefited from a considerable increase in the number of available posts as a result of this specialisation. Unfortunately, the pressure for specialisation and the expansion of special services has increased the likelihood that these services will become isolated from mainstream, generic services, with people having to accept a particular label before they become eligible to receive those services. Rather than improving integration this is likely to lead to further segregation. Those professional groups which have benefited directly from such segregation are likely to find it genuinely difficult to work for integration into generic services. An alternative would be to allocate extra resources to generic services so that people with a mental handicap could receive improved support from a more appropriately integrated source. In practice there is some evidence that without very strong controls imposed on the use of such resources, they are more likely to be used to meet alternative local needs judged to have a higher priority, often because they have a higher profile or a louder voice.

The move towards 'community care' may be seen by many ordinary, reasonable people as an expensive way to provide a home for people who already have most of their relatively meagre needs met in institutions. When their own way of life is far from extravagant, they find proposals for individuals with a severe mental handicap to have their own house or flat, with fitted carpets and an automatic washing machine, difficult to justify. All their own hard work, in a society guaranteed to produce inequality, has left them with a quality of life well below that which proponents of the normalisation principle would be prepared to accept for their clients. Normalisation has served to highlight a number of ethical, personal and political dilemmas but has so far failed to provide their solution. Societies which encourage and support, or impose a wide range of inequalities amongst individuals, must continue to live with the problems which result.

The evolution of any species demonstrates that there is usually a complex balance between the survival of the individual, the group, and the species as a whole. The human species has evolved into complex organisations which struggle to attain such a balance. In times of war or natural disaster the survival of the group is often achieved at the expense of individuals. Many individuals deliberately place themselves at risk to protect the group and the society in which they live. This raises their standing and they are declared to be 'heroes', thus increasing the possibility that others will behave in similar ways to protect the group during future disasters. Every culture transmits this basic value of putting the group interest above that of the individual through a set of myths and stories, as well as through its regular daily channels of communication. In recent times (for example, the Falklands War) the media, particularly some newspapers, and many ordinary people in their normal social interactions, exemplified this.

The apparent balance between individualism and the general interest of society has been the end-product of the market economy. It is argued that many people pursuing their own self-interest will guarantee a society which takes account of the general public welfare. This belief has produced the present society in which selfishness, competition and greed no longer guarantee the survival of the group, let alone the species. A simple example, quoted by Porritt (1984), is the use of common grazing land designed to be shared to the benefit of all. If one farmer attempts to graze more animals to improve his or her own interests, this will have little effect. As more farmers start to do the same, however, this eventually will lead to overgrazing which will destroy the common resource and will benefit nobody. True self-interest cannot be protected by each individual attempting to achieve short-term gains. Only by caring for others, for society, and ultimately the planet, can long-term self-interest be protected.

Societies need to convince their individual members that their own self-interests will be better served by moving towards a more sustainable way of life. The present situation, in which all governments, of whatever persuasion, the unions and the media combine to promote a way of life which relies on materialism, mass consumption and a virtual absence of concern over waste and pollution, will threaten everyone's long-term survival. Survival of the species is clearly linked to the behaviour of individuals and to the way those individuals in turn shape their societies. People need to learn that wealth at an individual level can no longer be measured in terms of the standard symbols of an affluent western society. In a sustainable economy, wealth will be measured by the degree to which people work and produce their own entertainment and food, taking responsibility for their own and their community's actions and achievements while reducing waste, pollution and built-in obsolescence. The transition to such a society will be difficult and will be achieved by many individuals understanding and working together. It will need government action to make the short-term consequences for individuals sufficiently positive to encourage them to move towards longer-term goals leading to a sustainable society. The validity of this argument can no longer be ignored by those supporting the normalisation principle for devalued people: they cannot simply maintain the status quo.

Chapter two

From consensus to conflict: the impact of sociological ideas on policy for people with a mental handicap

Andy Alaszewski and Bie Nio Ong

The Mental Deficiency Act (1913) established an administrative and legislative framework for the care and control of 'mental defectives'. This framework was based on a number of people with a mental handicap; mental deficiency was thought to be an objective property of individuals and, given the correct specialist and medical procedures, it was relatively easy to identify. Mental deficiency was thought to be inherited and institutions should form the corner-stone of any service designed to care for and control 'mental defectives'. Researchers using sociological ideas have successfully undermined the assumptions on which these policies were based. Mental handicap is not an objective entity but is a social category which depends on specific ideas and practices. Researchers have challenged the importance of heredity as a cause of mental handicap and drawn attention to the importance of communities both in establishing mental handicap as a problem and in providing resources for people with mental handicap. Researchers have undermined confidence in the utility and efficiency of institutions to the point that institutions are now 'the problem'.

Although researchers have successfully undermined the basis of traditional policies for people with mental handicap it will be argued that they have not replaced them with a simple integrated structure of ideas. In so far as a major policy initiative has emerged, it is 'community care', but this has a variety of meanings. It will be argued that feminist ideas represent a developing critique of the various conceptualisations of community care.

This chapter concentrates on policy as ideas. It adopts a traditional top-downward view of policy and sees policy as formulated by and within central government, to be implemented through the structures of various local agencies and the actions of local service providers. The relationship between sociological ideas, as embodied in research, and policy ideas, as embodied in policy statements, will be studied. This relationship can be direct and overt, as when a major piece of research has a clear impact on a specific policy statement. Usually the relationship is indirect and difficult to identify; a series of research projects creates a climate of opinion and this then informs the attitudes of policy-makers.

The chapter will discuss how research based on sociological ideas has in turn influenced policy. Each section will include a discussion of the development of the sociological ideas, followed by a review of research in the area based on these ideas, and finally a review of the influence of the ideas on policy.

Labelling people with a mental handicap

The Mental Deficiency Act (1913) created a legal framework for the care of 'mental defectives'. Central to this framework was the process of ascertainment: the identification and labelling of individuals as 'mental defectives'. The ascertainment procedure was modelled on other legal procedures. It involved the courts, the legal profession and legal judgements and a change in the social status of an individual certified under the Act. The decision-making was seen as relatively straightforward. It was accepted that a properly qualified specialist, in England a medical practitioner, had sufficient knowledge and skill to identify correctly the objective signs of 'mental deficiency'. The procedure was based on a clinical model of deviance.

In the 1950s and 1960s sociologists began to challenge this model of deviance. In the clinical model the identification of deviance and 'deviants' was seen as a straightforward business and deviant behaviour was a product of the innate characteristics of deviant individuals. Sociologists, however, argued that in practice it was difficult to distinguish between deviant and non-deviant behaviour. Similar actions could be classified in very different ways depending on social context and societal reaction. These sociologists emphasised the social processes or societal reactions involved in creating deviance.

This emphasis on societal reaction in the creation of deviance marked an important shift in the focus of sociological research. Rather than asking how much crime, deviance, disease or handicap existed, researchers asked how, and in what circumstances, did a behaviour or activity become defined as criminal, deviant, or evidence of disability, such that the person became labelled as 'criminal', 'deviant' or 'mental defective'. By rephrasing the problem, the centre of research interest shifted from the 'victim' and his or her characteristics to the agencies that defined specific problems, gave these problems names or labels and prescribed certain actions in response. Rather than mechanically and automatically responding to problems and individuals 'out there', the police, magistrates, doctors and psychologists were seen as playing an active part in the way social problems were defined and therefore created. Becker defined this approach when he stated that 'social groups create deviance by making the rules whose infraction constitutes deviance, and by applying those rules to particular people and labeling them as outsiders. From this point of view, deviance is not a quality of the act the person commits, but rather a consequence of the application by others of rules and sanctions to an "offender". The deviant is one to whom that label has successfully been applied; deviant behaviour is behaviour that people so label' (Becker, 1973).

The 'societal-reaction' model suggested that the process of labelling an individual as a deviant was an important social process that could have profound repercussions on the individual and literally change him or her into a different person. Individuals labelled as deviant would, for a variety of reasons, conform to a specific societal stereotype of a deviant and thus experience a loss of status or gain a social stigma. This new perspective on deviance was quickly used by researchers working with people with a mental handicap. In an early collection of papers edited by Becker, Dexter discussed the 'politics of stupidity' and argued that these people with a mental handicap suffered especially badly from a societal reaction: 'there is ... the experience which may be observed over and over again of the denial of employment, of legal rights, of a fair hearing, of an opportunity, to the stupid because they are stupid (e.g. have a low IQ or show poor academic performance), and not because the stupidity is relevant to the task, or claim, or situation' (Dexter, 1964). He argued that these people were discriminated against because they challenged the basic values of industrial society such as the importance of intellectual excellence.

The societal-reaction perspective on mental retardation found its clearest expression in the work of Mercer. Mercer was involved in a major programme of research into mental retardation funded by the National Institute of Mental Health in California. She joined the project to study the families of mentally retarded people and to conduct research into the problems of mentally retarded people responding to the stress and normal crises of life in a neighbourhood. The research rapidly ran into the problem of defining who was 'mentally handicapped' and it was transformed into a study of the ways in which mental retardation was created by various agencies.

Mercer started by identifying two separate perspectives on mental retardation, the 'clinical' and the 'social system' perspectives. 'The clinical perspective classifies mental retardation as a handicapping condition, which exists in the individual and can be diagnosed by clinically trained professionals using properly standardized assessment techniques. The social system perspective classifies mental retardation as an acquired status. Like any social status, that of mental retardate (*sic*) is defined by its location in the social system *vis-à-vis* other statuses, and by the role prescriptions that define the type of performance expected of persons holding the status' (Mercer, 1973).

The implications of the social system perspective were, as Mercer made clear, radical: 'If a person does not occupy the status of mental retardate, is not playing the role of mental retardate in any social system, and is not regarded as mentally retarded by any of the significant others in his (*sic*) social world, then he is not mentally retarded, irrespective of the level of his IQ, the adequacy of his adaptive behaviour, or the extent of his organic impairment' (Mercer, 1973). She found that state schools played an important part in the process of identifying and labelling 'mental retardates' in California. The behaviour and skills of a child played a part in the process of labelling, but equally important was the child's social status. Children with the same skills but different social backgrounds could be labelled and treated in very different ways. The closer a child's background was to the dominant anglocentric or white Anglo-Saxon Protestant culture the less likely that child was to be labelled 'mentally retarded'. Mercer argued that existing diagnostic methods, especially IQ tests, discriminated against minority groups.

Mercer's study had a number of policy implications. She noted that individuals were labelled 'mentally retarded' for a number of reasons. However, official agencies tended to treat this heterogeneous group of individuals as if it was homogeneous. For example, education pro-grammes were based on the assumption that all individuals classified as 'mentally retarded' had a low potential for learning. Mercer's recom-mendations drew on the contemporary civil rights movement. She emphasised civil rights and liberties of citizens, whether they were handicapped or not, and drew attention to the right of individuals to have equal opportunities and equal treatment. Specifically, Mercer argued that individuals had the right not to be classified as 'mentally retarded' merely because their social background happened to be different from that of the dominant social group. Labelling and classifying people as 'mentally retarded' should not be based on one single assessment such as the IQ test but should be based on a variety of procedures. Specifically individuals should only be classified as 'mentally retarded' if all the assessment procedures indicated they were retarded in their development. The research team experimented with this type of pluralistic evaluation and found that it halved the number of children classified as 'mentally retarded' and reduced the social discrimination against minority groups. The concept of pluralistic evaluation was adopted as part of the Californian legal system in 1971 (Mercer, 1973).

The right of individuals not to be labelled 'mentally retarded' was the dominant theme in Mercer's study. However, there were associated rights for the group of individuals who were still so labelled. Mercer did not discuss these in detail but emphasised that individuals so labelled should not experience a disadvantage as a result of labelling. They should have treatment and facilities appropriate to their circumstances which should be designed to help them return as quickly as possible and as much as possible to the norm. They should not experience treatment and facilities that were inferior to those experienced by other people and which could emphasise and maintain their status as 'mentally retarded'.

The societal-reaction approach to deviance also found a sympathetic audience in British researchers. Townsend, in his foreword to Morris's *Put Away* (1969), argued that the process of classifying mental handicap was dependent on social and cultural factors; that IQ tests were not culture-free; and that children of middle-class parents had an unfair advantage when tested. He also argued that many people classified as 'subnormal' and 'severely subnormal' had either not been properly assessed or 'their intelligence test scores considerably exceed the limits normally accepted for the purposes of definition by psychologists' (Townsend, 1969).

In policy terms, the societal-reaction model drew attention to the discriminatory nature of labelling and the deprivation experienced by people with a mental handicap in various segregated facilities. The emphasis was on desegregation and integration into 'normal' services. This movement has taken many forms and one pervasive name for desegregation is 'normalisation'. In the USA this movement was associated with the writing of Wolfensberger and with the work of the

Eastern Nebraska Community Office of Retardation (ENCOR) (Thomas *et al.*, 1978; Stark *et al.*, 1985).

Wolfensberger's starting-point was deviance. Societies could manage deviance in four ways: through the 'destruction of deviant individuals, their segregation, reversal of their condition or prevention thereof' (Wolfensberger, 1972). He argued that the first two techniques were unacceptable and harmed people with a mental handicap whereas the prevention and reversal of deviance were acceptable and desirable goals for society and the basis of normalisation. This involved altering both the deviant individual and his or her social environment so that he or she no longer appeared abnormal. The concept of normalisation formed the basis of a series of publications by the Campaign for Mentally Handicapped People (CMH, Kendall and Moss, 1972).

Policy statements by central government departments and various working parties and committees have, since the mid-1950s, stressed the importance of integration of people with a mental handicap into services provided for the general population. However, there has been an important change in emphasis. Early policy statements, such as the Report of the Royal Commission on *The Law Relating to Mental Illness and Mental Deficiency* (1957) and the White Paper *Better Services for the Mentally Handicapped* (DHSS, 1971), incorporated a weak version of integration. They emphasised the rights of people with a mental handicap to use services provided for the general population but the bulk of their practical recommendations was related to the development of 'specialist' facilities. More recent policy statements have provided a stronger definition and have suggested that services for people with a mental handicap could be integrated within generic facilities. For example, in education, the Warnock Committee (1978) recommended the integration of children with special needs into the mainstream.

The Jay Committee (1979), an inquiry into mental handicap nursing, was influenced by the concepts of integration and normalisation. Previous reports had started with a review of current services and practices and then made suggestions for incremental changes in the pattern of service provision. The Jay Committee took a more radical approach and started with a philosophical discussion of the rights of people with a mental handicap and then proposed a model of care. Their first principle emphasised the right of individuals to a normal life: 'Mentally handicapped people have a right to enjoy normal patterns of life in the community' (Jay Committee, 1979). The model of care was based on the principles of integration and stressed the rights and value of people with a mental handicap. 'The two groups of principles [on a normal lifestyle and on individuality] ... involve value judgements about the human rights of handicapped people in society .... It is important that the service system we develop should not be based on historic accident, that it should help the community to accept differences in their peers rather than reinforce prejudices' (Jay Committee, 1979).

The Committee was aware of tensions between the different ways of defining mental handicap and found them difficult to resolve. For example, in discussing people with a severe mental handicap, members of the committee held two views: either they wanted to categorise people into special groups or sub-classes, or they wanted to see each person as a unique individual with special needs and any classification was viewed as arbitrary, producing undesirable consequences. The Committee resolved this disagreement by avoiding the 'categorisation of special groups'.

Comment

Academics and researchers who examined existing service provision and organisational practices in the 1950s and 1960s challenged the bases and assumptions of these organisations. Sociologists, using a societal-reaction model of deviance, argued that deviance was not an innate characteristic of an individual but was the result of a complex set of social processes. Agencies did not discover mental handicap, they created it. Furthermore, the process of labelling individuals as deviant could and did create further disabilities for the 'deviant' people through an associated process of stigmatisation. Deviant people were separated from the rest of society and given an inferior position, from which it was difficult to escape.

The implication of this view was that, as much as possible, individuals should not be labelled 'mentally handicapped'. However, if they were to be labelled, they should not be excluded from the services received by the rest of the population but should benefit from these services. Any extra services they received as a result of their disability should enable them to return, as quickly as possible, to the life enjoyed by the rest of the population.

Although it is possible to identify these ideas in successive policy documents, the precise meaning and significance attached to them has changed. In early reports a fairly weak interpretation can be found.

People with a mental handicap were not to be excluded from services provided for the rest of the population. In later statements the interpretations were stronger. A positive attempt was to be made to integrate people with a mental handicap into society and detailed proposals were given for this integration to occur.

The genesis of mental handicap; the role of society

The authors of various policy statements before the Second World War were confident that they had identified the main cause of mental deficiency. It was thought to be inherited and consequently the defect was likely to be restricted to specific social groups. The solution to the mental deficiency 'problem' was thus a form of social engineering. The 'problem' and individuals had to be properly 'policed'. Through a programme of ascertainment, local agencies were expected to identify the problem neighbourhoods and the 'defectives' within them. They were to supervise the activities of these 'defectives' and segregate the most difficult and dangerous of them in institutions or colonies, especially those likely to reproduce and create a new generation of 'defectives'.

The relative pessimism of policy-makers fitted well with the contemporary sociological thinking about the nature of groups of people in society. At the end of the nineteenth century, sociologists detected the collapse of traditional forms of social organisations, especially local neighbourhoods, and noted their replacement by associations of individuals held together by mutual interests.

Tönnies, a German sociologist, contrasted traditional 'communities' with 'modern associations'. He argued that the traditional community provided an intimate, satisfying experience for its members, whereas the modern association was merely a combination of individuals held together by self-interest (Tönnies, 1974). There is in Tönnies' writing, as in that of many of his contemporaries, a strong element of romanticism. There are also assumptions that industrialisation had disrupted the fabric of society, destroying traditional communities and bringing social and personal degeneracy. Traditional communities were seen as caring, whereas modern society was seen as a collection of individuals, a crowd of strangers, in which each individual was concerned only with his or her self-interest.

In the 1930s and 1940s sociologists, especially in the USA, began to study 'communities'. The technique was pioneered in a study of

Middletown (Lynd and Lynd, 1972) which set the trend for subsequent community studies. The community study showed that neighbourhoods were not usually made up of strangers but contained social networks. Neighbourhoods could and did provide networks of support. Indeed, more care and support was provided by these networks than by formal agencies funded by the state. For example, in the study by Whyte (1955) of an Italian slum, important mechanisms of social cohesion and mutual support were identified.

In Great Britain, Young and Willmott conducted a major study of family and kinship in East London, in a traditional working-class area, Bethnal Green. This was compared with a new housing estate, Greenleigh. The former was a traditional community; individuals were born into it, lived in it and died in it, identified with it and were bound to it by a whole range of relationships. Young and Willmott identified the relationship between mothers and daughters as the key element in maintaining the cohesiveness of the community and argued that this bond linked three generations together in a mutually supportive network: 'In a three-generation family the old as well as the young both receive and give services; the aid is reciprocal' (Young and Willmott, 1957).

Young and Willmott compared this with the family life of individuals who had been rehoused in a new housing estate. They argued that the transfer broke traditional ties and relations. They concluded that the migration dislocated the structure of family relations and therefore impaired the caring capacity of people: 'It seems that when the balance of the three-generation family is disturbed, the task of caring for dependents at both ends of life, always one of the great and indispensable functions of any society, becomes less manageable' (Young and Willmott, 1957).

These community studies showed that networks of mutual support did exist within an industrial society. The studies also suggested, however, that these networks were restricted. Some people could draw on better networks, and some neighbourhoods were more supportive than others.

Parallel with sociological studies which identified and examined networks of social relationships, epidemiological surveys studied the nature and distribution of health problems within social groups. These studies supported the sociological research by focusing on, and emphasising the importance of, neighbourhoods in the creation and management of some health problems.

Armstrong (1982) argued that the development of routine surveys of health in neighbourhoods was associated with the development of dispensaries and health centres in the 1920s. The health centres had a radical impact on perceptions of disease and disability. Whereas disease and disability previously had been viewed as a biological malfunction of the body, experienced by a few individuals, they came to be seen as processes affecting whole communities. There was no clear divide between the normal and abnormal and therefore everybody was potentially diseased or disabled; for example, at a pioneering health centre in Peckham only 7 per cent of those surveyed were defined as healthy (Armstrong, 1982).

Epidemiological studies became a major part of medical science after the Second World War and they confirmed the importance of the neighbourhood in both creating and managing health problems. Whereas community studies indicated the possibility of improving the caring capacity of local neighbourhoods, epidemiological studies indicated the importance of controlling disease by improving the local neighbourhood.

Sociological ideas had an impact on the predominant view that 'mental defect' was inherited. On the one hand, researchers and campaigners using epidemiological techniques could find little evidence of heredity as a cause of mental handicap, and on the other hand sociologists began to identify the positive contribution of families and the neighbourhood to the care of people with a mental handicap.

If mental handicap was an objective, inherited, medical condition then it should be easy to identify the causes of the condition. When researchers looked at populations in specific mental handicap hospitals they found little evidence of a systematic and large-scale hereditary component in mental handicap (Leck *et al.*, 1967). Furthermore, 'mental deficiency' rates appeared to be age-specific. The National Council for Civil Liberties (1951) cited evidence that the ascertainment rates for mental deficiency reached a maximum of 30 per 1,000 individuals at age 12 and then declined to 8.4 per 1,000 individuals aged between 20 and 29. As there was no evidence of a differential death-rate, this implied that out of 30 individuals who were classified as 'defective' when they were 12, over 20 would be classified as 'normal' by the time they were 29. This evidence fits well with ideas described in section one of this chapter, especially labelling theory.

In mental handicap the impact of these studies was to draw attention to the importance of the family and the community in caring for people with a mental handicap. A good example of this approach was Bayley's study of the care of people with mental handicap in Sheffield at the end of the 1960s. He started from the ideological position that not only were most people with a mental handicap cared for at home, but by definition this was the best place for them. 'The futility of even thinking of creating a service apart from the community (in the micro-cosmic sense) is shown by the elderly. Over 94 per cent live at home and the vast majority live at home because they want to. Here, as clearly as in any branch of the social services, we can see that the community caring at the small-scale, face-to-face level is and must be the basis on which all services depend' (Bayley, 1973).

Bayley found that official agencies, such as local authority social services departments, were trying to replace rather than supplement care by families. He recommended a major revision of policy and practice: 'It is not a question of the community "supplementing official services"; it is a question of the official services helping and enabling the community to do better the caring it does already, with more help and less strain on individual members of it' (Bayley, 1973).

Assumptions held by policy-makers about the causes of mental handicap shifted as a result of research findings. The authors of the 1971 White Paper emphasised that the causes of most mental handicaps were unknown. Heredity was a factor, but only one amongst many. Mental handicap was a misfortune (*sic*) that could occur within any family and within any social group (DHSS, 1971).

Associated with changing assumptions about the causes of mental handicap were changing attitudes to the family and the neighbourhood. Rather than being subject to scrutiny and control, the family and its associated neighbourhood were to be the main source of care. This shift in focus was first evident in a fairly weak, *laissez-faire* form in the *Report of the Royal Commission* on *The Law Relating to Mental Illness and Mental Deficiency* (1957). The 1971 White Paper was more positive in the acknowledgement of the role of the family. 'Most parents are devoted to their handicapped children and wish to care for them and to help them to develop their full potential. About 80 per cent of severely handicapped children and 40 per cent of severely handicapped adults – and a higher proportion of the most mildly handicapped – live at home. Their families need advice and many forms of help, most of which at present are rarely available' (DHSS, 1971).

The Jay Committee made a much stronger ideological commitment to family care. It argued that the family played a key role in the life of people with mental handicap and that it should form the starting-point and focus of any service. In particular, the Committee felt that children with a mental handicap had a right to live in a family (Jay Committee, 1979).

Comment

At the beginning of the twentieth century, attitudes towards people with a mental handicap were shaped by a pessimism about the development of society in general. Many people, including sociologists, believed that order and stability in society was collapsing, and some believed that inherited mental defect was a cause of this collapse. To prevent further damage, a programme of social engineering had to be initiated which would break the cycle of degeneration by preventing the reproduction of mental defectives (*sic*).

Community studies contributed to the development of more positive attitudes. They showed that the social structure was changing and, in some respects, the new patterns of living were worse than the old. However, neighbourhoods and the family were both resilient and could provide considerable support for people who were ill or dependent.

In the field of mental handicap, there was little evidence that families 'caused' mental handicap or made the situation worse. Indeed, very much the reverse was the case. Families provided the bulk of care, often with little support from formal services.

Official policy statements showed a gradual recognition of the importance of the family. Initially, this was demonstrated by the *laissez-faire* position of the Royal Commission which could be summarised by the statement: 'families are caring, let them get on with it'. The 1971 White Paper represented an acknowledgement of the role of the family. In the Jay Committee Report the family was seen as the ideological core of any service.

The assault on institutions

The centrepiece of services established in the 1920s and 1930s was the mental deficiency colony. Colonies were to be repositories of all difficult people and the bases for active programmes of ascertainment and supervision. The Wood Committee (1929) believed that a comprehensive colony system, with a capacity to contain (*sic*) 100,000 inmates and to supervise a further 200,000 people in the 'community', would provide an answer to the mental deficiency problem.

One of the clearest impacts of sociological ideas has been to demolish the belief in the efficiency of institutional care. In 1961 an American sociologist, Goffman, published his seminal book, *Asylums*. Goffman worked for a time as a recreational therapist in a large American institution. Drawing on his experiences and on the extensive and diverse literature on different types of institutions, ranging from concentration camps to monasteries, Goffman created the concept of a 'total institution'. The total institution was cut off from the rest of society. As inmates were admitted, they were ritually stripped of all links with the outside world. Inside the institutions there were two separate and mutually antagonistic cultures: a dominant staff culture and a submissive patient culture. The institution was a mechanism of subordination and control, the apparent incapacity and dependency of inmates a product of institutional life and an essential feature of its operation (Goffman, 1961).

Criticism of specific types of institutions was not new. Since the Second World War, a number of British researchers had identified the debilitating and damaging effect on inmates of different types of institutions. For example, Lady Allen (1945), a distinguished voluntary worker, had exposed the unimaginative and depersonalising treatment of children in children's homes. Barton (1959), a psychiatrist, had written a training manual for nurses in which he argued that many of the patients in the long-stay wards of British mental hospitals suffered from two 'illnesses' – one related to their admission, and a second created by their stay in hospital. Goffman suggested, however, that problems were not limited to one specific type of institution, or to one specific client group, but were shared by all institutions and their inmates.

There followed a number of British studies that drew on Goffman's analysis and offered empirical support for his views. Townsend (1962) examined residential facilities for elderly people. Morris and Morris (1963) produced a sociological study of Pentonville Prison that described the effects of the exercise of power in the institution and related it to the inmates' social and personal deterioration.

The work of Goffman influenced two major studies of hospitals for people with a mental handicap (Morris, 1969; King *et al.*, 1971). In Morris' research, a team visited a national sample of thirty-five mental handicap hospitals. In each hospital they administered detailed questionnaires about facilities and care. The report of the study was published in the same year as the Committee of Inquiry into Ely Hospital and demonstrated that the specific failings and shortcomings in patient-care identified by the Ely Inquiry could be found in many other hospitals. Morris concluded that 'There are many things wrong with our subnormality (*sic*) hospitals, conditions in some places are Dickensian and grotesque' (Morris, 1969).

In the introduction to this report, Townsend offered a theoretical explanation for the shortcomings and inadequacies reported by Morris. Townsend argued that the segregation of people with mental handicap was the result of a desire to create clear-cut boundaries between the 'normal' and 'abnormal'. The hospital created the boundaries between normal and abnormal by stunting the development of people with a mental handicap. 'Patients' in hospitals were treated as subnormal. They conformed to these expectations and appeared to the outside world to be subnormal. Like Morris, Townsend defined community care mainly in terms of developing small-scale residential provision (Townsend, 1969).

King *et al.*'s study of residential facilities confirmed many of the findings of the Morris study. The research was part of a child-welfare project and the researchers were interested in examining the effect of different types of residential facilities on the management and care of children. Using Goffman's work, they developed a child-management scale which differentiated between child-orientated and institution-orientated environments. Using this scale, they compared child-management practices in children's hostels, voluntary homes and mental handicap hospitals.

The researchers found important differences between child-management patterns in mental handicap hospitals and hostels. The hospitals were institution-orientated and managed by complex hierarchies. Unit heads had little contact with residents, and many of the features of Goffman's total institution, such as depersonalisation and block treatment of 'patients', could be identified. In contrast, hostels tended to be child-orientated with far less emphasis on hierarchy. Unit heads tended to be closely involved in resident care. Hostels tended to provide a warm and homely environment. Residents tended to be treated as individuals and unit staff shared many activities, such as eating meals, with residents. Both Morris' and King *et al.*'s studies identified the large mental hospital as a major problem and both advocated the development of locally-based, small residential units.

The role of researchers was not limited to the examination of existing facilities. Tizard has been involved in an experiment to develop a small residential unit for children with mental handicap run as a residential nursery rather than a nursing home. He reported on the Brooklands Unit in his study of *Community Services for the Mentally Handicapped* (1964). Results of the experiment were very favourable; young children with mental handicap admitted to the unit, from traditional hospital care, made marked and significant improvements when compared to children in a control group who remained in the mental handicap hospital.

The concern about the quality of services for people in large institutions and the search for alternative forms of residential accommodation were recurrent themes in policy statements. The first official statement was in the Report of the Royal Commission (1957). Existing residential care was provided entirely by hospitals and the Royal Commission recommended that local authorities should develop a parallel system (Royal Commission, 1957). It was stressed that these residential homes should be small local units of twenty to thirty places and not more than fifty places.

The authors of the 1971 White Paper were preoccupied with the problems of the mental handicap hospitals. This was hardly surprising as the White Paper was published in the middle of a spate of scandals in such hospitals. Broadly, the White Paper accepted the findings of, and built on, contemporary research work. The White Paper acknowledged that large-scale institutions could be dehumanising (DHSS, 1971). It recommended an immediate ban on the construction or expansion of hospitals of over 500 beds. Similarly, a rapid expansion of parallel networks of local authority residential homes was suggested. The local authorities had been directed by the Minister of Health in 1959, and were obliged by the Mental Health Act (1959), to provide a full range of community services, including residential facilities. The White Paper found progress had been slow.

The policy proposals of the Royal Commission and the White Paper were incremental. Both started with existing services, examined their shortcomings and then made remedial proposals. Both reports identified large-scale institutional facilities as the major problem, and recommended the development of small residential units in the community as the alternative. The Jay Committee (1979), in contrast, adopted a more radical approach. It started with the rights and needs of people with mental handicap, developed the framework of a service that would respect rights and meet needs, and then examined the changes needed to create such a service.

The Jay Committee took for granted the criticisms of institutional care and therefore did not repeat them in its report. However, it did note that these problems were not restricted to large, isolated institutions but could also develop in small residential accommodation. The Committee, in contrast to the Royal Commission and White Paper, did not advocate an uncritical acceptance of local authority residential homes as an alternative to mental handicap hospitals. In the words of the Committee, 'A purpose-built unit on the outskirts of a housing development of a town is not in our view "in the community"' (Jay Committee, 1979). The Committee wanted all new residential facilities to be in houses organised in the same way as ordinary homes and to be as small as possible. They also felt that all people with mental handicap should have the right to live in domestic houses.

Like the Royal Commission and the authors of the White Paper, the Jay Committee emphasised the view of 'community care' as the provision of residential facilities in local settings. Unlike the previous reports, the Jay Committee envisaged all residential facilities in local settings and left no role for the traditional mental handicap hospital. It was also more specific about the nature and form of the residential facilities it wanted in the 'community', specifying adapted private houses.

Comment

Policy-makers at the beginning of the twentieth century believed that not only was mental defect relatively easy to define and its causes fairly obvious but also that the solution to the problem it posed was relatively straightforward. The construction of institutions was advocated as a repository for all 'difficult' people and as a base from which to identify and monitor the progress of all people with mental handicap.

Such confidence in the institution rapidly evaporated until it has become an accepted view that the institution, rather than being part of the solution, was really part of the problem. Although it has been relatively easy to define institutions as part of the problem, the solution to that problem has remained elusive. Despite official commitment to run down and even shut institutions, this has not happened. Institutions continue to take the lion's share of resources and it has proved difficult to move either residents or staff into new settings.

Community care and feminism

Sociological ideas and research have played an important part in undermining the assumptions behind the administrative and legal framework established by the Mental Deficiency Act (1913). However, agreement on an alternative framework has proved elusive.

In so far as an alternative has emerged, it is 'community care'. However, there is no precise and agreed meaning of community care. For example, a group of officials in the DHSS recently reviewed policies for the development of community care because there was 'some uncertainty about the general policy objectives underlying the concept of community care' (DHSS, 1981). The authors of the report acknowledged that the term '"community care" seems to mean very different things depending on the context in which it is used'. Part of the confusion arises because the three main schools of sociological ideas, which have informed critiques of previous policies, have also contributed alternative definitions of community care.

The critique of policies which developed out of labelling theory and associated ideas was based on the view that, as far as possible, individuals should not be labelled. If they were labelled, then, they should not be excluded from services provided for the rest of the population. The additional services that they received should enable them to gain access to the normal patterns of life enjoyed by the rest of society. This view of community care emphasises desegregation and integration of people with mental handicap into the community.

The critique which developed out of community studies was based on the view that formal agencies should not supplement or replace family or neighbourhood care but, as far as possible, should support them. It is a view of community care as care by the family and community.

The critique which developed out of studies of large-scale institutions was based on the view that they were intrinsically bad and damaging to their residents. By fostering dependency, institutions created the very problem they were supposed to solve. The solution proposed was to close institutions and, where necessary, to replace them with small, home-like residential units. This is a view of community care as care in the community.

Feminist ideas offer not only a general critique of community care but also a critique of these three alternative definitions.

Feminism is a more recent development than the three main schools of ideas discussed in the first three sections of this chapter. It has come to occupy a central place not only in sociology but also in other social sciences and humanities. Like most sociology, feminist sociology is concerned with the formation of, and relation between, social groups. However, unlike most other sociologists, feminist sociologists argue that one type of social grouping is evident in all societies and is fundamentally important to these societies. These social groups are based on the gender of group members. They argue that not only are these groupings important in all societies but that they have been neglected in sociological research.

Amongst feminist sociologists there is a difference in emphasis on the relationship between gender-based groupings and other forms of social groupings. At one end of the spectrum of opinion, radical feminists argue that gender-based groupings, roles and relationships are the dominant form of social organisation and refer to dominance by males (patriarchy) as the main oppressive force in contemporary societies. At the other end of the spectrum, Marxist feminists argue that gender relationships and conflict are only part of the wider class struggle between the owner of the means of production and the workers. Between these two extremes, some socialist feminists acknowledge the importance of social groupings based on both gender and social class. They argue that class struggle and gender struggle are equally important and that the allocation of resources within society is based on the way that these two forms of social conflict interact. Sociologists working within this framework, and using this perspective, have contributed most to discussions about the role of women as carers in a capitalist society.

One result of this feminist perspective was a renewed interest in the family, especially in the gender roles in the family. Mainstream sociologists investigating the structure of the family in the 1950s and 1960s identified a blurring of the paid-labour market with women leaving the household to go to work, and men becoming more involved in household activities such as child-care.

Feminist sociologists questioned these research findings. Oakley (1974) argued that most studies of gender roles in families used an asymmetrical model of the division of household labour as a baseline. Any variation from this asymmetrical baseline was then cited as

29

evidence of a trend towards a more symmetrical and egalitarian allocation of activities within the household. She argued that 'only a minority of husbands give the kind of help that assertions of equality in modern marriage imply'. The participation of husbands in a variety of household activities was examined. She found that conjugal role-separation was the dominant pattern in her sample of families. Sixty per cent of men had low levels of participation in domestic tasks, 45 per cent in child-care activities and 43 per cent in decision-making and leisure activities. Only 15 per cent of men had high levels of participation in housework and 25 per cent in child-care. Even in marriages which were egalitarian in respect of some activities, such as leisure and decision-making, there were often areas of inequality.

Oakley also examined attitudes to appropriate male and female roles. Most of her respondents, both male and female, felt that women should take prime responsibility for the home and the children. She was extremely sceptical of arguments that marriage was becoming more of an equal partnership.

Following Oakley's pioneering work, a series of studies found that the division of domestic labour is unequal and that women provide most of the care for children and elderly people (Ayer and Alaszewski, 1984; Nissel and Bonnerjea, 1982; Wilkin, 1979). The ideology of family life and the division of labour in the family produces and reproduces this differential time-allocation; women are allocated the tasks of providing for health, nursing the sick, teaching about health, mediating with health and social services and generally coping with crises (Graham, 1984).

Feminist sociologists have argued that the unequal division of labour is found, not only in the family, but also in the wider workforce. Women are represented in the workforce predominantly in part-time and lower-paid jobs. Their work outside the home is generally considered as secondary to their responsibilities at home, while the provision of child-care and support for dependent relatives are such that the development of a career for women becomes very difficult. State intervention is clearest in the area of social security benefits (Land, 1978). Critics of social security policies argue that these policies are based on the fallacious assumption that women, as wives, are dependent on their husbands, overlooking the fact that in contemporary society most families need two wages. The system of benefits contains disincentives for women to work, and women are not compensated for loss of earnings. This is most clearly demonstrated by the fact that until recently married women could not claim invalid care allowance. This has recently been successfully challenged in the European Court.

Although some recent research focusing on the care of people with a mental handicap has been influenced by feminist ideas (Ayer and Alaszewski, 1984), the main thrust of feminist research in this area has been on the implications of policy for women as carers. Viewed from a feminist perspective, community care is not care by, through or in 'the community' but care by women. In each of the separate meanings of community care women are expected to take the strain. In the view of community care as care by the community, it is the family, or rather women at home, which is expected to provide the bulk of the care. Not only are they seen as a relatively cheap resource but their lost career and work opportunities can be disregarded. In the definition of community care as care in small, neighbourhood units it is once again women who are expected to provide the bulk of cheap labour.

Community care, as a critique of institutional care, has been developed mainly as a family model of care (Dally, 1983). There is an implicit assumption that all forms of institutional care are bad, and life in a nuclear family is both desirable and normal in contemporary society. The view of community care as the integration of people with a mental handicap into local neighbourhoods is closely associated with the concept of normalisation in mental handicap. In this philosophy the dominant model of normality is also that of the nuclear family, in which the husband plays the economically active role and the wife is the carer for the dependent children in the household. Both models can be subjected to the same criticisms: nuclear families are neither normal (only 15 per cent of British families conform to a strick definition of this model) nor is it clear that they are necessarily desirable, when viewed from a woman's point of view.

In reality, women often have to earn a living outside the home and therefore they have a double role or burden as main carer and as wage-earner. Caring for dependent people is often seen as second-rate work that is accorded low status and low rewards. Feminist sociologists argue that only when caring for people with mental handicap is acknowledged as 'real work', and adequately supported materially and emotionally, will community care be a real alternative to institutional care.

The Social Services Committee of the House of Commons (1985) report on community care is one of the first in which the central role of families and mothers in providing care is seriously acknowledged.

Many witnesses have told the Committee of the sometimes intoler-
able burden of care that is placed on the families of mentally ill and
mentally handicapped people who are living at home. Constant
demands may exact a heavy toll on families, and particularly on
parents. According to the Social Policy Unit at the University of
York – 'The community care of young mentally and multiply impaired young adults involves arduous and unremitting physical work
and watchfulness, similar to the care and supervision needed by a
young child but extending over a lifetime and becoming increasingly
onerous as both parents and the young person grow older. Despite
this growing burden, there is no evidence of any involvement by the
wider community – friends, neighbours, volunteers or even extended
family members – in providing any of the care which is needed from
day-to-day. Instead, the burden of care falls largely on the young
person's mother and results in marked financial, physical and
emotional costs.'

The Committee felt that the needs of these carers had been badly
neglected and recommended that they should become a central focus in
future planning:

Community care depends heavily at the end of the day on relatives
caring for their own family members. There is a danger that the
establishment of new and expensively staffed services will produce a
continuation of the present relative neglect of families caring in the
community, to their personal and financial cost. We recommend that
all community care plans provide a statement of their impact on
families caring for mentally disabled relatives and specify the actions
to be taken in consequence.

Comment

The development of sociological ideas in the 1960s had an important
impact on services for people with a mental handicap, both directly
through research and indirectly through generating a climate of opinion.
This impact was greater in demonstrating the inadequacies of traditional
policies than in generating alternatives. There was a general agreement,
however, that 'community care' would provide a better service.

Feminism has had a radical impact not only on sociology but also on
a range of other academic disciplines. Feminist sociologists view
community care as care by women. They argue that the main burden of

caring for dependent people has always fallen on women and in so far as community care does involve any substantial changes it will reduce the rewards and support received by women and increase their responsibilities.

Although there is little evidence of a direct impact of feminist ideas on official policy, the climate of opinion has become more critical of community care. This is clear in the Social Services Committee Report (1985). Although the Committee endorsed the principles of community care it was critical of its practice. In particular, it acknowledged that families, and in particular mothers, provide the bulk of care for dependent people and they have received few benefits from the policy. The Committee argued that the needs of carers must be urgently addressed.

Conclusions

This chapter has reviewed the impact of ideas on social policy for people with a mental handicap. Ideas are elusive. They can be difficult to define and their histories and influences are often difficult to identify. This chapter has defined and identified four major sets of sociological ideas; it shows that these ideas have successfully undermined existing or emerging policy for people with a mental handicap but that they have been less successful in informing alternatives. In the past thirty years the consensus over policies has been replaced by confusion and competition.

Generally, this confusion and competition is regarded as bad. Service providers often yearn for the golden era in which there was a simple design for services which was embodied in a government statement and implemented by a government agency. The Mental Deficiency Act (1913) embodied such a design and services developed for nearly fifty years along the lines laid out by that design. The only problem was that the design was wrong.

'Community care' has not provided any alternative grand design or single plan. Perhaps there is no real advantage to centrally-inspired design. Services for people with a mental handicap will develop most effectively if central government gives a firm commitment to provide funding and encourages local agencies to experiment sensitively with services. If such experiments are effectively evaluated, especially in terms of the ways in which they meet the needs of people with a mental handicap and their families and carers, then a better pattern of services will develop.

Chapter three

The importance of relationships

Martin Jackaman

This chapter considers some of the relationships that both exist and need to be made to improve services offered to people with a mental handicap and their carers. Although the network of services has improved over recent years, fundamental attitudes to mental handicap have changed marginally. There is more public awareness than ever before, but there is not necessarily more public acceptance; and some age-old prejudices and fears still exist. It is against this backcloth that the services have to be built and developed. It is in this context that the person with a mental handicap and his or her family live. Relationships have to be made to build bridges between professionals, parents, family and society. People with a mental handicap will also need relationships with their peers, and with health, education, housing and social services staff. These represent some of the bridges required in working with people who have a mental handicap. Such bridges can provide shelter and support for people with a mental handicap and their parents, and a starting point from which to plan for the future.

What types of services are needed?

In discussing the appropriateness of the service, practical and emotional needs facing parents and their child with a mental handicap need to be considered. Various crisis points will occur from the immediate implications of 'diagnosis' to the death of parents, and associated changes.

Receiving news about the presence of mental handicap or disability can be a devastating experience, following a time of joyful anticipation [and also dormant fears that a child may be abnormal]. Indeed, diagnosis may be in doubt for weeks or months and those giving the 'news' may not be trained or skilled in this practice. At this time of uncertainty, parents need to talk to someone who can not only be aware of their feelings of deep loss, anger, failure, resentment and guilt, but can also talk honestly and sensitively about what resources and help are available. When parents feel able to discuss the future of a person with a mental handicap, they need answers about what can be expected.

The practice of breaking the news requires skill and sensitivity. Worthington (1984) notes:

> Those who felt that they had been dealt with honestly and sympathetically, remain very grateful to the doctor for his (*sic*) respect for them. They left the interview feeling that they were on the same side, so did not feel brushed off or resentful .... Many parents, however, felt exactly the opposite. In addition to their confusion about the child's handicap they came away with a burden of anger, embarrassment and a sense of hopelessness.

Similarly, Cunningham (1979) reported: 'Some said that they were not told soon enough, that husband and wife were not together, that there was no attempt to ensure privacy when given the diagnosis and they were not given enough information.' In this research only 20 to 30 per cent of parents were told of the diagnosis together. Moreover in 50 to 60 per cent of the cases, one spouse was left to inform the other. If professionals seeking to help parents at this crisis time are unable to establish relationships with each other and with the family, not only is adjustment seriously affected, but also parents may lack confidence to seek outside help in the future. Often, in later years, professionals trying to help families have had to deal first with parents' past experiences, before working with the current situation.

The ability of professionals to establish relationships with each other and to use their knowledge and expertise is paramount to meeting parents' needs. The need for accuracy in medical diagnosis, knowledge and information includes counselling and other issues, such as the way staff respond at this difficult time. It is crucial to create an environment in which both positive and negative feelings can be expressed. These should be tackled by medical staff, nursing staff, health visitors and social workers as an interdisciplinary team. There is often an implicit assumption that the ability to impart medical knowledge also qualifies a physician to be a skilled counsellor. However, as Russell (1985) notes: 'This is no easy task, and it requires the availability of someone whom the parents can trust and who is in a position to cope with anger, grief and despair which will inevitably emerge. Such individuals are often difficult to find'.

By including the parents in this team, a network of support can be provided which will sustain carers, and form foundations for a supportive service to be available whenever it is required. Cunningham (1979) notes the 'shock phase', showing itself in emotional disorganisation, confusion, paralysis of actions, disbelief and irrationality. This can last from minutes to days and is usually followed by the 'reaction phase'. Various expressions of sorrow, grief, disappointment, aggression, anger, denial, guilt, failure and the use of various defence mechanisms may occur. Parents need someone at this time who can listen, understand, cope with anger, be honest and not be deterred by the negative aspects of this phase. The parents can then move into the 'adaptation phase' and begin a realistic appraisal when they ask about the future. This may lead to the 'orientation phase' when parents begin to organise, seek help and plan for the future; regular help and guidance are required.

During these phases parents make contact with professionals within both health and social services. Professionals should understand the behaviour of parents who may seek a second medical opinion, or project their anger on to those seeking to help. The involvement of physicians and social workers is itself a reminder of the presence of a child with a handicap. The great need for skilled counselling at this time requires a senior practitioner with experience in counselling to cope with the negative aspects of adjustment. In addition, counsellors require status within the service structure to work closely with other senior staff and to begin to co-ordinate their involvement in helping parents. It is also necessary to tackle the emotional needs of grandparents, brothers and sisters, all of whom may need skilled counselling and practical support.

The development of a clear policy on how parents should be informed and by whom, should be accompanied by the establishment of a network of support workers. Sustained support should continue until relationships can be developed within local neighbourhoods. One study (Cunningham *et al.*, 1984) showed that improvements in how parents were informed about the presence of a mental handicap or disability increased satisfaction with services. Procedures were developed by which parents of a baby with Down's syndrome could be informed. The sharing of information was as follows:

1 diagnosis was given by the consultant paediatrician (if possible with a health visitor present).
2 as soon as possible after the birth of the baby.
3 both parents were told together.
4 information was given privately (with nurses or students not present).
5 information was given with the new-born infant present, unless seriously ill.
6 information was given directly and parents were given time to ask questions.
7 parents were informed that the health visitor would see them again.
8 parents were given a private place immediately after the interview, where they could talk without the risk of interruptions.
9 twenty-four hours later, a second interview was arranged with both the consultant paediatrician and health visitor.
10 parents were informed that a psychologist would visit them within six months of the birth, to complete a psychological assessment.

To achieve this kind of response it is necessary to have a clear policy. Physicians should work together with health visitors and social workers. The extensive nature of counselling requires the involvement of a social worker. If a team approach is used, however, it may be appropriate that other staff adopt the key worker role in the long-term maintenance of support to the person with a handicap and his or her carers.

There is a need for relationships to be established between professionals as an interdisciplinary team, both in institutions and in local neighbourhoods. Parents and professionals should also establish relationships in order that they may work together; and a strong relationship between the parents is useful as a mutual source of help. Relationships between the institutional and neighbourhood services are also required if parents are to receive help once they begin the task of caring for their child with a mental handicap in their own home.

The value of parent groups should not be underestimated. The social worker may be essential in the establishment of parent groups and may provide support in several ways, utilising both casework and groupwork skills. Conflict between professionals may be counter-productive at this time, when people need to be clear about their roles. Some have expertise in sharing knowledge; others are skilled in the 'management' of the child with a mental handicap, or in dealing with the emotional issues that face parents. This expertise should be used in a combined effort to tackle the situation. Parents may require a period of 'mourning', simultaneously with caring and planning for the needs of their child. It is combining the many aspects of the task that can make this process extremely demanding. As Mittler (1983a) noted: 'Whatever we do, our approach has to be flexible, tolerant and open to change'.

The early years

Possibly the most important aspect of the service is the relationship between 'institutional' staff and neighbourhood workers. It is useful to clarify what is meant by 'community team'; this is usually a small team, serving a population of 80,000 people, which typically consists of social workers, community nurses and other professionals such as pre-school teacher–counsellors and specialist health visitors. There may be access to physiotherapists, psychologists, occupational therapists, speech therapists and other consultants. The main task of these teams is to work with the day-to-day problems and possibly also to undertake development and education work. They are frequently accommodated in an identified building and work closely with the primary health care services, social workers and domiciliary services staff in the local social services offices.

Demands for services of the child with a mental handicap in the early years are varied, including the often unexpressed wish of carers to share negative and positive feelings and fears. They need someone to be available to help with their emotional adjustments; decisions need to be made between 'institutional' and 'neighbourhood' services about particular roles. Similarly, other services are required for the day-to-day care of the child with a mental handicap, for early stimulation, and for counselling of other close family members. For the team workers there is the wider aspect of educating society if parents are to be assisted with 'the second handicap' – that is, other people's reactions to their child with a mental handicap.

The question of education is the responsibility of professionals working both in mental handicap teams and in day-care or residential work. As McConkey and McCormack (1983) have noted: 'Education can never be a single entity or a catalyst effecting change, in disabled people and most significantly of all, in the professional services for them'. This can only be achieved when education is no longer viewed as extra work done occasionally by specialist staff. Rather, it should be an integral part of every service caring for people, irrespective of the presence of disability, impairment or handicap.

Neighbourhood workers should address the issue of education through work in schools and should take advantage of the wider opportunities available through a more effective use of the media and other direct contacts. Parents and the person with a mental handicap could themselves be involved in discussing problems that arise in breaking down the existing barriers to effective communication. One way of doing this is by using personal contact with people who have a mental handicap. More positive integration attempts amongst school children are necessary, if attitudes are to be changed. Unfortunately, whilst mental handicap continues to be confused with other disabilities, particularly by the media, it can be an uphill struggle to reverse the misinformation of members of the public.

In the early years the service quality depends on the professionals that make contact with the family. This requires extensive relationships at different levels, as parents may have contact with institutions, assessment units and the mental handicap team members. The team should work collectively, towards agreed objectives. The pre-school teacher–counsellor and health visitor need to enable the child to receive the necessary stimulation and develop his or her potential. Working together as a team may help to bridge gaps that might otherwise lead to second-rate services.

The issue of 'special education' can be extremely difficult for parents as it is a stark reminder that their child is not considered by others to be 'normal'. The relationship which the social worker and other team members develop with colleagues in education (the pre-school teacher–counsellor and the special school staff) can help to reduce parents' concern at this critical point. The involvement of other parents can also give support, as they can answer some of the questions which carers may wish to ask at this stage in the life of their child with a mental handicap. As Warnock (1978) notes: 'The successful education of children with special education needs is dependent upon the full involvement of their parents'. This statement may be theoretically sound; however, parents only have a certain amount of emotional energy and often need additional help to deal with their feelings.

At this time 'separation' should be discussed within a supportive environment. Some parents will require 'sitting schemes', by which a person who has appropriate training can stay in the home, so that the person with a mental handicap (or their carer) can become mobile.

Similar schemes, such as 'shared care', allow parents to have a recip-rocal arrangement with other carers, thus enabling them to have planned breaks. It is, however, rarely easy for parents to allow another person to care for their child without experiencing feelings of guilt and ambi-valence; therefore they should be given ample opportunities to discuss this early in the child's life. Parents who feel unable to allow this to occur should have their feelings respected, although it involves a conflict of interests. Above all, parents should have choice and services should be available to create real choices. Services should not simply provide short-term care facilities to offer relief, but should also help parents to allow someone else to care for their son or daughter. This area demands sensitivity and understanding, and the ability to appreciate the emotional conflict that parents experience when making such vital decisions. The use of other carers at this time can also provide support to families. Parents experiencing similar difficulties can share their feelings to gain mutual support.

Despite sensitive counselling by professionals who have established trust, this can be damaged if the response is insensitive when parents first meet the residential staff or the fostering family. If this occurs, parents will be likely to seize the opportunity to say, 'not just now, thank you'. Relationships between teams, schools, parents, people offering relief-care and professionals should be based on mutual respect, or the person with a mental handicap and their family will experience unneces-sary psychological trauma. In these early years, the increased use of parent groups may be of value to families; professionals should therefore learn to work alongside such groups.

The teenage years

Research on the difficulties experienced by an adolescent with a mental handicap and his or her family is sparse. It is the time of transition and change; there is general acknowledgement that the shift from the protection of childhood to the responsibilities of adulthood can be particularly difficult for the adolescent who has a mental handicap, and can also be a very testing time for family members or carers. The question of leaving school and making choices requires that adequate information is available about the range of options for work, leisure, continuing education, future residential care and support services. For parents it is a particularly difficult time; as Marks (1980) notes: 'The hopes and aspirations of the early school years may be unfulfilled and there looms ahead the adult training centre, which may seem dull, unattractive and repetitive by comparison to the school'. The structure of training centres has given new focus and direction to adult services, and change is required when parents often have established strong relationships with schools and the education services. Suddenly they may find, at a time when they most need help (when physical and emotional changes in their child are making life more difficult), that now they have to operate in a new environment. There may also be confusion as to whether certain problems should be resolved by adult or child services.

A divided service is of no use to families; one strength of a mental handicap team should be that it does not reject families at this time. It can provide one of the few consistent supports as the transition is made from child to adult services. Relationships need to be established between the team members, schools and the work place, if a smooth transition is to be accomplished for the person with a mental handicap. Similarly, relief schemes require continuity and consistency so that disruption is minimal. Neighbourhood services should work in close liaison; the co-ordination of health, education and social services needs to be improved in order to reduce barriers that exist between specialist schools and adult services. In the present structures, a child may often risk loss of friends by moving into an adult training centre. Children may see their friends in the neighbourhood outside school hours; this is unlikely to happen to children with a mental handicap unless they meet at Gateway Clubs or other specialist activities.

The adult years

For most parents one central question has been unanswered since they were told they had a child with a mental handicap: 'What will happen to my child when I die?' As their son or daughter attains adult age the answers to this question become imperative. Many elderly parents cope with this question with the hope that their son or daughter who has a mental handicap will not outlive them. Many single parents find this dilemma extremely worrying. Attempts to make provision for their son or daughter's future before they die often involve confrontation of further parental loneliness and despair. Equally, if they do not plan for the future, then further guilt and uncertainty may occur.

Ambivalence, guilt and the question of death, frequently concern elderly parents; the ability of professionals to work with these feelings depends on a sensitive approach. Relationships are required between people working in the neighbourhood and those in the residential services who offer care for the future. Parents need ongoing counselling, even when their son or daughter has left home. This may occur especially in situations of emergency, for example, when parents enter hospital as a result of an urgent admission due to ill-health. A bridge is required between the older parent and professionals who will provide care for the son or daughter.

Summary

From the time of initial diagnosis through to adulthood, there are numerous practical and emotional events for both the parents and the person with a mental handicap to resolve. These events may not be traumatic but may be times of stress which underline that parents do need the help of other carers and professionals if they are to successfully complete these stages in the life of their son or daughter. Services, therefore, should be established to respond in a flexible and, above all, sensitive way.

Future services – critical aspects of relationships

Present services are fragmented between health, education and social services. Likewise, a division exists between child and adult services. Unified services, which might be considered desirable, are difficult to achieve. Within the social services, there is a tension between generic and specialist services. Some people favour the generalist approach which responds to all client groups. Moreover, a number of social services departments operate separate child and adult services within the generic model. There is, however, a continuing trend to return to specialist workers under the auspices of area social services offices, but located in a separate building, with members of the inter-disciplinary team.

This latter approach acknowledges the importance of strong relationships between services, if professionals are to give the maximum support to the person with a mental handicap. Generic workers often are not skilled in mental handicap services and may find it more difficult to develop close working relationships with other professionals. The division of child and adult services may also be problematic. This could mean that, rather than providing a consistent approach as families readjust to using adult services, at every stage new relationships are required. At the time of adolescence, the wisdom of creating a division amongst those persons supporting a family should be questioned. Close working relationships with the area team are vital to fully utilise the resources of social services departments, such as domiciliary services, to finance parent groups and to have some degree of integration into generic services for children or people who are elderly. In some instances these generic services will be more appropriate for a particular family or person with a mental handicap. Developing wider neighbourhood links to make maximum use of departmental resources such as research and information should also occur.

One of the benefits of an interdisciplinary team is that by working together at a local level within the health, education and social services, workers can help to unlock some of the organisational structures within their agencies. Through close working relationships, barriers can be broken down and bridges built between parents and professionals. This, in turn, encourages the growth of parent involvement in the development of services.

Working in this area requires consideration of the practical and emotional needs of parents, brothers, sisters, grandparents, as well as the child or adult with a mental handicap. Responding to the person with a mental handicap whilst ignoring the feelings of those who care for them should be avoided. Social workers should acknowledge the development and progress of the person with a mental handicap as well as recognising the parents' need to come to terms with their feelings about having a child with a mental handicap. Visits that professionals make within the home should focus attention on the needs of the person with a mental handicap and also on those of the carer. Similarly, it is an error for professionals to talk with carers and not to recognise the presence of the person with a mental handicap in the same room; active involvement of both parties is a prerequisite for positive relationships.

In planning future services the separate practical and emotional needs of the carers and those of the person with a mental handicap should be acknowledged. Divisions also exist between child and adult services and the problem of integration into society requires resolution. A wide range of services is required: counselling to meet emotional needs; practical help, such as short-term care; residential facilities; and befriending schemes allowing social life to flourish. Services should be planned to meet the needs of the child, and to facilitate communication, mobility and planned risk-taking. In taking risks, close work with parents is essential to avoid unrealistic demands on either the family or the person with a mental handicap.

In enabling carers of the person with a mental handicap to lead a more independent life, it is crucial to develop a network of support within which all people can feel trust and mutual respect. The planning of future services to meet both family and individual needs requires consideration of the following dimensions, which should be part of any fully comprehensive service:

1 Initial assessment of disability (including diagnosis if relevant).
2 Effects of loss and emotional needs within the network of relationships.
3 Day-to-day life for the carers and the person with a mental handicap.
4 Enabling carers to allow the person with a mental handicap to receive care from other people, through the resolution of feelings such as guilt, ambivalence and separation.

In the early years paediatric services, in conjunction with the inter-disciplinary team, should develop a clear policy on how information is presented to carers within the interdisciplinary team. This may involve paediatricians, health visitors, nurses, and social workers, in provision of direct counselling and information to help parents to accept the birth of a baby with a mental handicap into the family. The use of parent groups can be particularly helpful. Relationships should also be developed with neighbourhood workers and paediatric services. Responsibility for care ultimately will be transferred to neighbourhood workers. Membership of the neighbourhood team has been the subject of much discussion. Teams should respond to the needs of both the parents and the person with a mental handicap, although conflicts of interest may occur. The functional needs of the person with a mental handicap require consideration of communication, mobility, skills training, health, counselling, and emotional development. This may require the involvement of speech therapists, physiotherapists, psychologists, teacher–counsellors, health visitors, nurses and social workers. On a theoretical level there are many components which together can form a co-ordinated service. In practice, however, the factors which determine the level and quality of the service are the relationships developed by workers. Availability of this professional expertise, together with the experience of parents, forms a useful focal point within any neighbourhood for help and support. The management of organisations determines whether or not this model of service delivery will be effective, or whether greater fragmentation will result from involvement of more people.

The role of the team in developing services

Whilst the development of local interdisciplinary teams can be of benefit in the provision of a 'front line' service to the family and person with a mental handicap, essential development work can be sacrificed for the apparently more immediate needs of individual people. At times services have been developed without a comprehensive evaluation of parents' wishes or collection of data to support the development of individualised services. In some social services departments working closely with health service workers, teams have been developed with a specific development brief to refer day-to-day issues to the existing area teams. In establishing priorities, comprehensive surveys have formed the foundation of the development work. Specific projects have emerged, such as the setting up of adult placement schemes, which can provide short and long-term substitute care for people.

Local play schemes have been developed in some services and some parents have been actively involved in the planning of these schemes. Parent groups have been established which have been the foundation of the development of more localised residential services. Following survey information, parents have formed pressure groups, with the help of a development worker, to create residential services within their own neighbourhood. Involvement of the parents in the identification, development and implementation of these schemes has been a feature in partnerships between parents and professionals. Establishment of 'personal relationship' and counselling groups and befriending schemes has resulted from the efforts of social workers specialising in development work. Health service workers such as speech therapists, psychologists, physiotherapists, nurses and occupational therapists have also been involved. The benefits of interdisciplinary work, and parent involvement in planning and developing services, have been vital in the process of establishing resources.

The interdisciplinary approach has helped to put into practice some of the theoretical aspects of working together. In planning future services, professionals need to supplement each other by working together as a team. Two examples illustrate this point. A man with a mental handicap who had been living with his neighbours for some thirty years in a small village was helped to remain in his home when his elderly carers moved into warden-aided accommodation. The occupational therapist completed an assessment of his social and domestic skills and worked with the team social worker, area domiciliary services and the housing department in order to maintain him in his own home. Similarly, a woman of forty with Down's syndrome wanted to stay in her own home after the death of her father. Adult training centre staff, working with a social worker, domiciliary services and the housing department enabled this woman to remain at home with the full support of her family. For both of these people an additional benefit of this experience was that they gained maturity, since the professionals worked together to enable them to develop an independent lifestyle. Failure to appreciate potential for partnership between professionals, particularly in the health and social services, may mean that a limited range of services are established for people with a mental handicap.

The development of good working relationships between professionals has been the corner-stone of the success of the development teams. Much more could be achieved, however, if there were other specialist local practitioners working with day-to-day aspects of life for people with a mental handicap. The benefits of locally-based interdisciplinary teams to resolve day-to-day issues illustrate clearly the deficiencies of teams that undertake little development work; such teams fail to influence policy development. Whilst local teams provide day-to-day services for the family, there is also a need for development workers to become part of the team. Alternatively, to develop a strong power base, they can become part of a central development team whose workers relate to particular areas within the health authority. Broader development work issues, such as the adult placement scheme and larger residential projects, can thus achieve a much wider perspective.

What kind of life?

Popular concepts such as 'normalisation' or 'integration' have formed the basis of thinking about the kind of life that should be established for the person with a mental handicap. Choice and 'fulfilment' should also be taken into account. The person with a mental handicap and his or her parents have a right to a range of services, from which they can choose those most appropriate to their needs. Alternatively, they can make an informed choice to reject the services. Whilst it may be desirable for the vast majority of people with a mental handicap to live in an ordinary house, for some people it may not be the most appropriate setting. Careful thought is required to avoid taking normalisation to extremes. The operation of any service requires personal freedom for both the person with a mental handicap and their family. Many parents, however, experience isolation from society. Services therefore should aim to prevent isolation by the development of reciprocal relationships between parents, professionals and wider society. Increased involvement of parents and the growth of self-advocacy also are essential developments. The growth of choice and partnership between parents and professionals should not, however, create unrealistic expectations in parents, making them over burdened with too many demands on their energies.

The preparation of a neighbourhood is a subject for debate. Many people favour early discussions with neighbours and key people in the local neighbourhood. Similarly, involvement of domiciliary services often requires that local people are regularly involved within the home of the person with a mental handicap and this can help to break down local barriers. Social workers and other professionals have a responsibility to develop services for individual people with a mental handicap, not only in terms of practical skills, but also in their emotional development and personal relationships.

A question of philosophy?

In establishing any group-living scheme, a clear philosophy and direction need to be determined, and the key worker should take overall responsibility for this. One problem is that many people involved in services for people with a mental handicap may be so preoccupied with success that they may work against the agreed philosophy, perhaps by 'doing' rather than by 'enabling'. A balance is required, particularly when budgeting for the daily running of the home of the person with a mental handicap. Ideas may have to be modified or challenged to allow people with a mental handicap to make informed choices, based upon previous experience and knowledge about probable consequences. Professionals therefore need to encourage full independence, rather than risk 'doing' everything for people with a mental handicap.

The adoption of a philosophy which constructively meets requests for professionals and others to enable the person with a mental handicap to take risks is more demanding. Domiciliary services should adopt a teaching role, rather than doing more than is required; people with a mental handicap may be at-risk from over-protection. Practical considerations should determine the policies adopted in provision of services. The establishment of reciprocal relationships is essential in running any successful group home; domiciliary services staff and social workers need to develop inter-professional relationships, as well as relationships with the people with a mental handicap.

Fieldwork data on this topic can be extremely revealing; people with a mental handicap who in the past have lost their parents previously have been placed in a hostel within twenty-four hours. This demonstrates how quickly the service system may produce an 'institutionalised' response, when other, more creative options are available. Frequently people have been left out of decision-making; even when they have been actively involved, professional interests have influenced the outcome. Even if a philosophy has been established that does not revolve around professional interests, it is necessary to provide continued support. Decisions may be taken by people with a mental handicap, but there is still a need for outside help and advice when situations occur which cannot be resolved immediately. In comparison with past experiences of residential care, there is now much greater freedom; however, this brings greater responsibility.

Professional power

The 'power' of professionals specialising in mental handicap can be abused. The degree of power that professionals exert in all aspects of work requires close monitoring. People with a mental handicap have the ability to live valued and fulfilling lives, with much independence, in local neighbourhoods. If professionals do not enable them to develop such lives, staff working with them can become isolated.

Under one roof?

The development of positive relationships is essential. People who provide services may be in danger of working in geographical and professional isolation. Co-ordination of services and shared relationships are crucial to avoid this danger. Interdisciplinary work in institutions and neighbourhood settings can succeed if positive relationships are developed between professionals. Workers, therefore, should appreciate that neither the institution nor the neighbourhood team can function efficiently unless they are working together with common objectives, using their own particular expertise to meet identified needs.

There is considerable suspicion amongst professionals about issues such as the value of social work and the power of the physician, but if these difficulties can be resolved, the benefits to the person with a mental handicap and their families are considerable. If professionals believe in common objectives, professional differences can be discussed, accommodated and, more often than not, resolved. Shared accommodation helps the different services to develop relationships between themselves, enabling departmental structures to be clarified as well as establishing positive links within the other organisations responsible for services.

Relationships between parents and professionals are also changing. Interaction between professionals and people with a mental handicap is no longer a one-way process. With the development of parent groups, greater involvement in planning, and the growth of voluntary organisations, the consumer can be placed in the forefront of the service. In addition, with the growth of self-advocacy schemes, the person with a mental handicap is able to take an active part in this process. Adults with a mental handicap may actively seek to develop relationships in their personal lives as appropriate. This two-way reciprocal relationship is essential and gives the person with a mental handicap something in return.

The increased involvement of parents in developing services to meet their expressed needs has shown that they can exert a significant influence in establishing local resources, by acting as a pressure group in neighbourhoods. Social workers have a role in developing relationships with individuals and their families. Their ability also to establish wider relationships with the range of services is crucial if they are to ensure that the best care is made available.

Sufficient finance to develop a service is difficult to obtain. There will always be differences of philosophy and direction about the services that develop. The responsibility is often divided amongst a number of services. A range of views should be considered: those of the person with a mental handicap, their carers and the neighbourhood. Professionals should work together to respond to the demands of the individual, family and neighbourhood.

The development of an interdisciplinary approach to enable the growth and involvement of both parents and people with a mental handicap is a welcome initiative. Sound working relationships may help to ensure service quality. Professionals should be prepared to learn from each other, to appreciate constraints and to plan more co-ordinated services.

The importance of relationships in creating valued services is essential. There is a need for 'warm, caring, stable and predictable relationships with which clients survive' (Atkinson, 1982). If the finances exist to develop a range of services, the quality of the service hinges on the relationship between the service-provider and the consumer within the wider framework of society.

Chapter four

Changing service systems: a contribution from research

Roger Blunden

Research and service systems

For more than twenty years public concern has been expressed about the position of people with a mental handicap. In Britain there has been a series of media exposures, often followed by committees of inquiry and government statements (e.g. Department of Health and Social Security, 1971). Mental handicap, in name at least, remains high on the list of priorities for government action to improve services. In Wales, there is now a national strategy, with some funding provided towards a major restructuring of services for people with a mental handicap (Welsh Office, 1983).

Part of this developing concern has been a recognition that the services provided for people with a mental handicap have often contributed to their problems. Various research studies have highlighted this negative impact of services. For example, Goffman's classic analysis of the negative effects of 'total institutions' (Goffman, 1961) was followed by empirical studies by King *et al.* (1971). Oswin (1971) has written moving accounts of the bleak existence faced by many children with a mental handicap in residential care, based upon her own detailed observations. Bayley (1973) studied the problems faced by families caring for a person with a mental handicap at home, and showed how services, where available, could often supplant rather than support families' efforts.

Various advances have been made in the design of teaching systems to enable people with learning difficulties to develop more effectively. Researchers have demonstrated the effectiveness of home-intervention services, ward-based activity periods, and other service components designed to provide practical help.

Although there have been many successful demonstration studies showing the effectiveness of particular service components, commentators have drawn attention to the lack of widespread implementation of such research. Mittler (1977) stated that 'considerable knowledge is available which is simply not being used for the benefit of handicapped people and one of our tasks in the immediate future is to plan systematically to bridge the gulf between potential and performance'. Baumeister (1981) asked: 'To what extent is [mental retardation] policy directly formulated on the basis of scientific knowledge?' and concluded that 'the answer is not very much'. Berkson and Landesman-Dwyer (1977) conducted a detailed review of research on severe and profound mental retardation and found evidence of substantial advances in care-giving and training methods. On the basis of this review they concluded: 'The knowledge that has been gained in the last twenty years provides the basis for improved services. Much has been learned by answering questions raised in practical situations. However, there is nothing in the literature to indicate how this knowledge has affected the delivery of services'.

Each of these commentators has acknowledged that, although there is considerable information about ways of delivering more effective services, effective strategies for implementing and sustaining change on a large scale do not exist. Much literature addresses these problems of implementation and maintenance. Repucci and Saunders (1974) listed a range of problems faced by those who attempt to implement new programmes. They concluded that the innovator requires a good working knowledge of the structures, goals, traditions and linkages present in the existing services in order to implement effective change. Boles and Bible (1978) reported the constraints operating against change within a residential institution, including the complexity of the system and the various pressures, inertias and conflicts which take place within it. They pointed out that a manager within such a system is faced with a problem of environmental 'repair'. The system is already there and needs to be changed, rather than there being scope for implementation of a totally new system.

The components of the service do not operate in isolation, and any attempt to change one will produce reactions and resistances elsewhere in the system. Linkages are present in a number of different ways. For example, different service components may share a common funding arrangement or be part of the same management structure. Clients may make use of a number of components at the same time, so there is a need for co-ordination. Office facilities or catering arrangements may be shared. This notion of services as complex systems has been developed by a number of authors from different viewpoints (see, for example, Blunden, 1984; O'Brien *et al.*, 1981), and is part of a wider movement to view human organisations in terms of systems (see, for example, Brethower, 1980; Checkland, 1981).

Researchers and others interested in promoting change have shown that isolated changes in individual components of services are likely to be ineffective. Change has to be directed towards entire service systems. The remainder of this chapter describes one attempt to develop and evaluate an entire service system containing a number of components. The exercise had a number of features often absent from a research approach to change. The project involved establishing an entire service system, containing a number of components of service delivery; researchers were involved in the design, as well as the evaluation, of the services; a long-term evaluation was built into the exercise, with regular feedback to encourage the service to respond to the results of the evaluation; considerable emphasis was given to the dissemination of results and good practice during the course of the experiment, as an aid to innovators elsewhere.

NIMROD – an example of a systems approach to change

In 1977 a unique opportunity occurred for researchers to become involved in the design and evaluation of an entire service system. Considerable discussion had taken place about the future of services for people with a mental handicap in South Glamorgan, with some pressure on authorities to replace existing, hospital-based services with a comprehensive, locally-based service with residential and domiciliary support provided for people living in their own homes, or in substitute homes in their own locality. In response to this pressure a compromise was agreed whereby proposals were completed for the establishment of a pilot locally-based service for a defined geographical catchment area of 60,000 population.

A working party was established by the Welsh Office, bringing together civil servants, representatives of the health and local authorities in South Glamorgan and members of the Mental Handicap in Wales Applied Research Unit. The task of the working party was to prepare proposals for a pilot locally-based service and its evaluation. Thus researchers were fully involved from the inception of the project and were able to make a substantial contribution to the working party report.

In the design phase, attention was given to a wide range of issues, including the way the service would relate to existing services and the wider service system. It was important that key people within the health and local authorities supported the introduction of the new service. Funding arrangements were discussed and agreed. Mechanisms were devised to help ensure that the new service would maintain a high level of quality and that standards would not drift.

The overall service system embraced three main subsystems:

1 the service delivery subsystem; a range of services were to be provided to people with a mental handicap and their families.
2 the staff support and quality control subsystem; it was important to clarify the roles of staff, to ensure that they received the necessary training and support, and to ensure that the quality of the service delivered to clients was maintained at a high level.
3 the project funding and management subsystem; the new service's links with existing agencies were formalised through a management committee comprising elected members of the participating authorities and a steering group of officers. A method of joint funding was agreed for the project.

In 1978, the participating authorities agreed to the establishment and funding of the new service, which was to be called NIMROD. During the next two years, considerable effort was directed into the detailed planning of NIMROD. Initially, researchers adopted a leading role in this process but, as the service co-ordinator and other staff were appointed, these took over the planning and implementation roles.

The NIMROD service is described in detail elsewhere (Mathieson and Blunden, 1980; Humphreys *et al.*, 1986). The following is an outline account of the three major subsystems identified above.

The service delivery subsystem

Within the overall aims of the service, a number of key functions were identified:

1 to ensure that services to every client were planned and delivered on an individual basis, drawn up wherever possible in close consultation with the client and his or her relatives, and reviewed

at regular intervals. A method of individual planning was established to achieve this.

2 to provide individual training and problem-solving. A goal-orientated approach was designed, whereby long- and short-term goals identified in the individual plan were divided into steps and implemented systematically.

3 to provide accommodation in ordinary houses in the local setting for people with all types and degrees of mental handicap. Various options were planned including staffed houses, group houses and a 'fostering and lodgings' scheme.

4 to provide support to people with a mental handicap and their families. A range of support services was planned including 'sitting-in'; an advice, information and resources centre; and short-term care on a planned and emergency basis.

5 to encourage volunteers and relatives to provide recreational activities for clients in the evenings and at weekends. Links were developed with voluntary agencies and consumer groups.

6 to facilitate access to existing services (both specialist and generic). A range of existing services was identified. It was recognised that, in many cases, these services were inadequate (or non-existent) and it was anticipated that NIMROD would help stimulate developments. In particular, it was recognised that day services for people with a mental handicap needed considerable development.

Most staffing resources were organised on a 'patch' basis. Four 'communities' of approximately 15,000 population were identified. Each had its own 'community care manager', two 'community care workers' to work with clients living at home and in the group houses, and a senior care worker and care workers in each of the staffed houses to provide the necessary support and training for residents.

The NIMROD Centre staff comprised a project co-ordinator (appointed at a senior level to facilitate communication with other agencies, decision-making and implementation), a senior social worker, a senior psychologist, an administrator and a secretary.

The staff support and quality control subsystem

The functions of this subsystem were:

1 to provide a clear specification of the duties of staff. A series of

procedural guides was written, outlining key duties of staff. It was envisaged that these would form the basis of staff training and support and that the guides would be modified according to the subsequent developments.

2   to train staff. A staff training programme was devised which would both introduce staff to the general aims and concepts of the service, and give them the specific skills necessary to follow the procedural guides.

3   to promote a high-quality service. It was recognised that, in the absence of clear guidelines and feedback, standards could slip and the service quality deteriorate. A number of checklists were drawn up, based on the key activities of staff, so that service quality could be reviewed via a process of 'positive monitoring'.

4   to support staff. A 'positive monitoring' system was envisaged as a method of providing staff with recognition for good performance, and constructive feedback where standards were not achieved.

The project funding and management subsystem

The functions of this subsystem were:

1   to ensure that funds were made available for the service. A method of joint funding was agreed between the Welsh Office, county council and health authority.

2   to ensure that the project survived, within the policies of the participating authorities. A management committee was established as a sub-committee of the county council, including members of the city council and health authority.

3   to ensure co-ordination between NIMROD and existing services. A steering group was established with senior representatives from the participating authorities. A senior practitioner group was also established to involve middle managers from these authorities.

Research on NIMROD

A programme of research was an integral part of the NIMROD proposals. The main aims of this research were:

1   to develop service components. Researchers made major contributions to the initial plans for the service contained within

the working party report. Subsequently, with the appointment of the co-ordinator, researchers wrote many of the procedural guides and completed preliminary plans for staff training. As more service staff were appointed, the research contribution to service development decreased.

2   to describe services as they developed. A *NIMROD Chronicle* was established in which both researchers and service personnel recorded major events and issues in the development of the services.

3   to measure the use of services. Consumers' use of both new and existing services was monitored for the duration of the research project.

4   to measure the impact of the service on its clients. A key feature of the research was to evaluate the effects that the new services had on users.

The main method for measuring the use of services and their impact on consumers has been a long-term evaluation study. The nature of the project produced a number of innovative features of the research. First, the time required to develop the service and fully implement it implied that the research would be lengthy. A six-year period was agreed, with additional time provided at the end for the completion of a final report. It was recognised from the outset that major time and resource commitments were required to complete a full service evaluation.

Second, a central problem in the evaluation of human services is the lack of agreement about what constitutes successful outcomes and how these can be measured. If a single measure of 'benefit' existed, widely accepted by practitioners and researchers, the tasks of evaluation would be comparatively simple. In real life, however, different people have adopted different criteria and measures of success. The present evaluation was based upon a multiple evaluation strategy consisting of four components (Irvin *et al.*, 1979). The four components were: a broad band-width measure of skill acquisition and performance; a naturalistic observation instrument; a rating of consumers' satisfaction with services; and an external evaluation using the Program Analysis of Service Systems (PASS) (Wolfensberger and Glenn, 1973). The first three of these components were incorporated into a strategy of regular data collection; the external PASS evaluation was planned to be conducted towards the end of the evaluation period.

The third unusual feature of the evaluation was the type of experimental design adopted. Two types of design previously have been used. Typically comparisons are made between an 'experimental' group of people who receive the new service and a 'control' group who do not. The second type of design typically involves measures taken before the introduction of the service with repeated measures taken afterwards. The evaluation of NIMROD afforded an opportunity to combine and extend both types of design into a multiple baseline time-series design, normally only used in single-subject research (Kratochwill, 1978). The NIMROD service was introduced into each of the four geographical 'communities' sequentially. A fifth 'comparison community', which would not receive the new service, was also selected. Measures were taken at regular intervals on all people with a mental handicap in each of the five 'communities'. This has made it possible to measure the impact of the introduction of NIMROD in each of its four 'communities' independently, and to compare it with results in the fifth 'community', where NIMROD has not been introduced.

The long-term evaluation of NIMROD and some preliminary results have been described. The analysis of the full set of data on clients of the service is now under way. An additional research component has been a series of short-term studies, designed to examine various aspects of the service in more detail than is possible in the long-term study. These have included a survey of NIMROD staff (Evans *et al.*, 1984), an examination of the effects of moving into a staffed house (Evans *et al.*, 1987) and a collaborative evaluation of NIMROD's system of individual plans (Humphreys and Blunden, 1987).

It is clear at this stage that considerable progress has been made in establishing the service delivery subsystem of NIMROD. A range of neighbourhood services is now available to people with a mental handicap in the project catchment area. Not all aspects of the original plans have been fully implemented, however. A number of clients who are eligible for services have yet to receive them. Some relatives have declined the offer of NIMROD services; NIMROD has not yet been able to provide suitable accommodation to all who require it; not all clients who require volunteers have yet received this service. Aspects of the staff support/quality control subsystem have also not developed as originally envisaged. Plans were being made for the management of NIMROD's services to become integrated with the two 'community mental handicap teams' now established in the west of Cardiff. This provides an opportunity for these aspects of incomplete service development to be reviewed. Nevertheless, NIMROD is a major example of the feasibility of establishing locally-based services for people with a wide range of mental handicaps.

Conclusions

This chapter has described one way in which research has been applied to the problem of establishing effective services for people with a mental handicap. From the outset a systems approach was adopted, with researchers recognising the need to design, implement and evaluate a 'package' consisting of service delivery, staff support and quality control, and funding and management subsystems.

Such an approach to service development is feasible in establishing a new form of provision. There is some evidence from early evaluation data that the service benefits some clients. There is also evidence of a more informed critical appraisal of the service by some families. The research is still being completed. However, two general lessons emerged at an early stage.

The first lesson relates to the approach to evaluation, involving repeated measures of the impact of services on individual clients over several years. This client-centred approach over a long time-period is an entirely appropriate way of evaluating such a service. However, during the research period, other ideas have developed about the nature of important dependent variables and measurement methods.

At the time of planning, the major focus for service development was on client skills. An effective service was thought to be one which enabled its clients to learn, use and maintain a range of skills appropriate to everyday living. Thus, in this study considerable emphasis was placed on the use of the Adaptive Behaviour Scale (Nihira, Foster, Shellhaus and Leland, 1975) as a major dependent variable measure. In practice it appears that the ABS is a relatively 'blunt instrument'. Significant changes in scores on any of its domains require substantial changes in behaviour. Similarly, many of the changes perceived by clients, parents and staff as highly significant for an individual (for example, increased 'confidence', reflected in opening the door and greeting visitors) do not register on the ABS.

Thinking about the aims of the services has also developed further. Interest is now focusing on clients' 'lifestyles' as a major dependent variable, rather than a simple focus on skill acquisition. For example, in a later project to evaluate the All Wales Strategy for the Development of

Services for Mentally Handicapped People (Welsh Office, 1981), five elements of 'lifestyle' were considered: community presence, relationships, choice, competence and respect. Thus the development of skills (as reflected by competence) is but one dimension of client outcome.

The second major lesson of the research relates to the extent to which it was possible to maintain the experimental design during a period of several years. The time-series design required a high level of control over the independent variables in the research. In this case this required tight experimental control over such aspects of the service as staff recruitment, training, monitoring arrangements and staff support.

In practice, the researchers adopted a major role in the initial design of these aspects of the service system, but as the service became established, the amount of influence exerted by the researchers diminished considerably. This was partly due to pressure from the authorities commissioning the research that evaluators should not 'interfere' in the course of the experiment. It also related to an understandable wish by the management of the new service to be allowed to develop in their own way without 'outside' interference. From the researchers' viewpoint, the considerable effort involved in conducting the evaluation left little time for complex negotiations over the detailed running of the service. The net result was that the contents of the service evaluated differed in many important ways from what was initially planned. In particular little emphasis was given to a 'competency-based' model of staff training and support which featured in the original plans.

The NIMROD experience has been an important source of learning for clients, families, service personnel, and researchers. It is still too early to 'stand back' from the experience and draw clear conclusions, but some tentative thoughts about the implications for future research are summarised as follows.

1   A research approach to service systems is worthwhile. If services are to develop with quality as well as quantity, there clearly should be continuing research directed towards the design, implementation and evaluation of service systems.
2   More thought is required about the dependent variables used in research. Since ideas about aims of services are changing rapidly, it may not be possible to adopt a system of fixed measurement over time. Some of the qualitative aspects outlined above may be

difficult to measure in valid and reliable ways. Considerable additional effort may be required to develop useful measures.

3   Additional effort is also needed to describe independent variables in the research. A service such as NIMROD is a complex system both in organisation and in interpersonal relationships. Methods are required to describe and 'untangle' some of the complexities. One promising possibility may be the area of 'soft systems analysis' (Checkland, 1972).

4   The issue of involvement of researchers in the service's process needs to be urgently resolved. If researchers are seen as 'impartial' observers, outside the service, then a different approach to experimental design and evaluation is required to that adopted here. If new developments are used as 'testing grounds' for new ideas in service design, then a clear partnership needs to be firmly established between researchers and service managers and the terms of this partnership made explicit from the outset.

Postscript

Since this chapter was first drafted, there have been major developments in both the NIMROD service and the associated research. Whilst the essential issues raised here remain important, interested readers are referred to the Mental Handicap in Wales – Applied Research Unit and to South Glamorgan Social Services Department for an updated account of research and practice.

Chapter five

Relationships in question: people with a mental handicap, their parents and professionals

Tim Robinson

The purpose of this chapter is to explore a number of dangers arising from an overenthusiastic and uncritical application of some of the new approaches to mental handicap. It will be argued that one safeguard against many of these dangers lies in improving relationships between professionals, people with a mental handicap and their families. This requires an examination of the existing barriers to an improvement in relationships and a discussion of ways to overcome them. The chapter will also consider some recent developments which affect the pattern of relationships between professionals, parents and people with a mental handicap.

Recent developments

The last twenty-five years have been associated with dramatic changes in society's approach to mental handicap. This has not always been 'the quiet evolution' that Lane has suggested (Lane *et al.*, 1983). At times it has been decidedly turbulent and there are plenty of signs that the turbulence will increase. The pervasive pessimism, the dominance of the medical profession and the emphasis on segregation which characterised the earlier years of the century have all been radically challenged from several directions. The criticisms and the alternatives proposed may not add up to a completely coherent approach but their effects have, none the less, been substantial.

Central to many of the changes has been new emphasis on a shared humanity with people with a mental handicap, together with a renewed optimism about their potential to learn and develop as people. There has been a growing emphasis on their rights as citizens. These factors, together with a recognition of the destructive effects of institutionalisation, the past lack of opportunities, and society's negative attitudes towards people with a mental handicap, have produced an emphasis on normalisation and integration into society. There has also been an acknowledgement of the importance of parents, both in bearing the bulk of the responsibility for care, and in influencing the way their children develop. This has stimulated a shift away from the traditional, one-sided relationships between professionals and clients towards a greater emphasis on participation and partnership. Even though progress has been patchy, these new developments have undoubtedly played an important part in improving the quality of life for many people with mental handicap and their families (Heron and Myers, 1983; Lane *et al.*, 1983; Mittler, 1979).

Some words of caution

The potential of these new approaches is real. The enthusiasm and zeal that often accompany them, however, are not without danger. Unless this danger is faced, the potential is unlikely to be fully realised.

Zeal can lead some people to become strident and intolerant of any disagreement or questioning. Ambiguities and contradictions within the new perspective may be minimised. Insufficient attention is paid to what is really happening to people as reforms are introduced. In short, philosophies, theories and structures which should have been liberating have begun to turn into prisons. Ironically Wolfensberger, as a key proponent of normalisation, has warned of just such a danger (Wolfensberger, 1969). He noted that in an earlier period, 1890–1918, when a different orthodoxy reigned, it was not possible to find a single voice raised against the prevailing view that 'the retarded' were a menace to society. In a telling aside, he went on to wonder what non-existent voice future reviewers would look for in vain in the current epoch.

Philosophy into ideology

The recent literature is replete with references to the need to involve people with a mental handicap and their families, and respect their choices, and the importance of taking account of the unique individuality of each person in working out how general principles should be applied. If these injunctions are fully honoured, the problems are not likely to be serious. At times, however, they seem to be little more than ritual incantations, with other passages in the same works spelling out a different message.

Heron and Myers, for example, in a generally sensitive discussion of recent developments, have been critical of the idea that adults with a mental handicap might remain in their parents' home. They suggested that the usual expectation in society is that people should leave their parental home by their mid-twenties. As a consequence, if people with a mental handicap remain in the parental home beyond that age, it will be as a 'permanent guest' in the home of a previous generation. In such a situation, they argue, there will be no doubt about whose home it is and who makes the decisions (Heron and Myers, 1983). Clearly, this argument is valid for many people. It does, however, ignore that some people who have not been labelled as having a mental handicap choose to live with their parents beyond their mid-twenties. They can often work out amicable and enriching arrangements in which the home is shared. Similarly, they write of all village communities which offer a long-term home as 'mini-institutions'. Tyne (1985) has suggested a similar view where anything short of full integration is dismissed as 'the new apartheid'. Significantly, he does not address any of the reservations that are expressed about his own position, but instead avoids debate by his use of the term 'apartheid'.

Even apparent expression of choice by people with a mental handicap themselves is sometimes dismissed and discounted. For example, it is not uncommon to find that some hospital residents resist offers to move into alternative accommodation and even adopt evasive tactics in response to programmes designed to prepare them for such a move (Gunzberg, 1975). Many people who initially resist such a move, however, change their minds after actual experience of life outside the hospital (Birenbaum, 1975). The danger is that this argument is then routinely used to discount all expressions of a preference for hospital. Only a few writers seem prepared to acknowledge publicly that, for a minority, hospital has become home and that perhaps they have a right to remain there (Mittler, 1979).

Alternatively, an individual's wishes may be discounted by emphasising the years of inappropriate learning experiences and blocked opportunities which have restricted many people with a mental handicap. O'Brien and Tyne (1981) took this view when commenting on the persistence of age-inappropriate behaviour in adults (e.g. carrying a teddy bear, or spending hours on a swing). They recognised that there may be conflict between supporting an individual's choice and trying to

substitute age-appropriate behaviour. Their answer was to discuss how
the behaviour could be subtly manipulated rather than crudely controlled by removing the teddy bear. They implied that the person's
apparent choice (holding the teddy bear) could be legitimately dismissed because it was based on 'inappropriate' learning.

Clearly such arguments for overriding the apparent wishes and
immediate feelings of people with a mental handicap have some force.
The danger is that they may be used in a way which hides the real
dilemmas involved. If these tensions and contradictions are not
addressed, it is possible that practices such as normalisation, integration
and personal development will be imposed on people with a mental
handicap, whilst it is denied that this is happening.

Theory into dogma

The new approaches are not simply about philosophical principles. They
also include theories of how to change both people with a mental
handicap and the rest of society.

Labelling theory has been used to justify the principle of normalisation (O'Brien and Tyne, 1981; Wolfensberger, 1972). The theory
suggests many of the problems experienced by people with a mental
handicap are the result of other people's reactions to those who have
been so labelled. These reactions are portrayed as overwhelmingly
negative and based on stereotypes which paint a misleadingly pessi-
mistic picture of the degree of incompetence and the problems
experienced by people with a mental handicap. The consequence is that
they are forced into stigmatised roles in society. Their self-image and
self-confidence are drastically affected and they are denied opportunities to develop more normally. This lack of development confirms
other people's negative view of them. Thus the labelling process creates,
or at least seriously exacerbates, the 'problem' of mental handicap.
Advocates of normalisation have been concerned to find ways to revise
these negative spirals and to make them benign (O'Brien and Tyne,
1981; Wolfensberger, 1972).

Unfortunately, perhaps because of the way that empirical and moral
justifications for normalisation have become entwined, proponents of
the approach have rarely evaluated its effectiveness. For example,
Wolfensberger talks about normalisation as both self-evidently valid (in
terms of current psycho-social theory research on deviancy, role
performance, etc.), as well as right (in terms of socio-political ideals),

(1972). When the moral and empirical become entwined in this way it is possible that people with mental handicaps become used as 'battering rams' in an effort to change society (Gunzberg, 1975).

There is, sadly, little evidence in the normalisation literature that its proponents are aware of recent re-evaluations of labelling theory or of the considerable body of evidence on 'teacher-expectation effects' (Schur, 1971; Plummer, 1979; Gove, 1980; Mercer, 1975; Gordon, 1980). Williams and Schoultz (1982) claim one self-advocacy project for example has shown that there is 'no limit to what people can do except for the limitations imposed by restrictive attitudes and lack of confidence'. The recent literature on these effects puts exaggerated claims like this into perspective without discounting the very real negative effects of some labelling. Theory must remain in touch with empirical evidence.

Problems may also arise with behaviour change techniques derived from behavioural and developmental psychology (Mittler, 1979; Clarke and Clarke, 1974). Precisely because such techniques are effective influences on behaviour, there is a temptation to use them without sufficient consideration for the person involved. As Anderson (1982) has noted, there is a real risk that both professionals and parents come to treat people with a mental handicap as objects.

In a milder form, there is a danger of placing the person in a permanent 'trainee' or 'student' role, perhaps through lifelong attendance at an adult training centre. Most people value a student role for part of their lives, knowing that they can choose to stop 'being developed' at some point. Precisely because effective learning methods are available, however, it is tempting to keep the person with a mental handicap in a permanent trainee or student role.

The need for humility

The issues discussed in the preceding sections involved complex dilemmas and difficulties. Two essential qualities in confronting these problems are humility and a readiness to discuss matters openly with people whose views are different. Unfortunately, the force of conviction which has provided the impetus to enable the new approaches to make a real impact has also encouraged the premature closure of discussion in many cases.

Without this humility and openness, the frequent references in the literature to the need to individualise the application of general principles and to involve people with a mental handicap and their relatives in decision-making are in danger of becoming merely empty rhetoric. How far they become reality, so that people are treated as individuals, will depend on the quality of the relationships professionals establish with them. In the words of O'Brien and Tyne (1981), these must become much more 'open, direct and sincere'. Unfortunately, there are some substantial barriers to achieving this.

Barriers to better relationship

Many people who are attracted to human services professions have a genuine concern for their fellow citizens. This concern helps in establishing the kind of open, sincere and direct relationships which O'Brien and Tyne have advocated. These relationships can help professionals develop an accurate understanding of how each client sees his or her own life and this makes service provision more individualised. The processes of professional socialisation (ways of thinking, styles of working) may, however, create barriers to clients. The pressures of work settings can add to these barriers. This section will explore several potential barriers to the development of relationships with clients and colleagues, which professionals are likely to encounter in their everyday work.

The socialisation of professionals is a powerful process which can significantly change those who experience it (Bucher and Stelling, 1977; Robinson, 1978). The process will affect: (i) people's view of the world, and of themselves; and (ii) their ways of relating to people seen as clients.

Professional training is concerned with teaching the relevant area of expertise to the student and inculcating a proper sense of ethical responsibility towards his or her work. This is clearly designed to be of positive benefit to future clients. It is, however, a Janus-headed process. The budding professional is likely to develop a strong personal commitment to his or her expertise which makes it difficult to accept other people's views as equally valid. The focus on the person with a mental handicap as a client who has come with a problem may exacerbate this situation. This can easily lead to a re-interpretation of the client's behaviour and viewpoints so that they are discounted. Some professional accounts of the parents of children with a mental handicap illustrate this well (Mathey and Vernick, 1975; Roth, 1974). The process continues into the professional's career as their views often become more cynical. The teaching profession describes this as 'chalkboard wisdom'. Each professional group has its own distinctive perspective and will approach clients from that perspective, believing that their approach involves the most salient aspects of the problem.

Cunningham (1983) characterised the more extreme forms of this problem as 'expertosis', a condition in which the victim's head swells and blindness rapidly develops. He goes on to identify some of its main symptoms: pre-empting parents' questions before they have had a chance to finish; stopping explaining one's actions, observations and analyses as one goes along; recognising increasingly familiar cues and using increasingly familiar recipes for dealing with them; and so on. In short, the professional has stopped listening openly to the parents and has ceased to pay attention to their individual views. This is not simply a problem that affects other people. It is the other face of professional socialisation and every professional needs to guard against its effects. The problem is likely to be particularly acute in work with people with a mental handicap (CMH, 1973a, 1973b).

The problem may be compounded by the ways in which professionals learn to deal with their clients. Professional time tends to be at a premium, so encounters with clients become confined to issues which are directly relevant to the particular professional's role and expertise. As a consequence, most professionals learn, overtly or covertly, to control encounters with clients. Whilst these techniques are necessary to effective work, they can also get in the way of the kind of open relationships necessary to an accurate appreciation of the client's life. If a true partnership with clients is to be achieved, perhaps through a key-worker role, professionals must stop controlling interviews and learn new skills. How far changes of this order can be effected without some aspect of the traditional work of professionals being adversely affected is unclear. It may prove necessary to divide the interview into different sections, so that for some of the time a traditional approach predominates, whilst in the rest of the time a more open, two-way dialogue is encouraged. This may be demanding for the professionals involved, but the benefits to the client might prove considerable. It will be necessary therefore to examine existing professional training to see how this might be influenced by the views of the client.

Concentrating on the client, methods are required to ensure that the client's voice is not lost in the preoccupation with learning professional knowledge and skills. Sessions which allow clients to speak to students are relegated currently to occasional, rather peripheral, events in the training programme. They may be seen as 'light relief' from the serious business of the course. They need to become a central part of the course; students should be encouraged to relate them to other parts in a systematic way. This might be done in a number of ways.

Clients could be invited to share their experiences and views directly with students and staff (Mittler and McConachie, 1983b). Where this is difficult for clients, autobiographical tape-recorded or video material can be prepared. Such material illustrates that the world looks different from the other side and has more facets than any particular professional perspective normally allows. Interpretation of the information into professional jargon must be discouraged. A second possibility is to arrange placements with clients. The aim would be to give students the opportunity of seeing clients' lives directly, without imposing a professional blueprint. These placements would depend on client agreement, but many people might be prepared to take part if they understood the benefits. Another possibility is the role-play exercise, in which the student takes the part of the client.

Unfortunately, initial training is only the start of the problem. If anything, the pressures to take a narrow view of the world (and of clients) increase as the student becomes a full professional. Students can easily become restricted by their own perspective, and too easily isolated from clients. Human service work requires regular periods when professionals are expected to take time out from their routine work with clients and to spend time simply listening to them. Conferences in Britain which brought professionals and people with a mental handicap together, in a neutral and pleasant setting to share their views, were a useful start. Although such conferences encountered a number of problems (CMH, 1973a), such opportunities are a valuable way for professionals to refresh their sense of their clients' views.

All of this will be of little use if professionals simply slip back into old styles of relating to their clients in their everyday work, which inhibit or discourage a more open dialogue. McConachie (1983b) has suggested that most professionals find it difficult to adjust to a more equal relationship with clients. It is important to identify the social skills required and to develop ways of teaching these. The use of techniques based on videotaped role-play, with informed feedback on performance, seems to offer particular promise in this respect. Such skills are too important to rely on them developing simply through experience.

Organisational preoccupations

Professionals are employed by large hierarchical organisations. These organisations affect the kinds of relationships which can be developed with clients. They have a variety of other concerns besides responding to the individual needs of particular clients. To survive or expand they should attend to their public image and to their relationships with powerful groups such as politicians, senior ministry officials and the media. They should also negotiate with a range of other services whose work borders on their own. Internally, questions of financial accountability, managerial control, smooth administrative functioning and departmental priorities may assume primacy. All of these impinge, directly or indirectly, on the relationships between front-line professionals and clients. The organisation may take time away from the work of building relationships with clients. Efforts to co-ordinate services may turn the professional to solving organisational concerns, such as rationing resources and resolving disputes about power and boundaries, at the expense of the quality of service to clients (Ferlie *et al.*, 1984).

The professional may begin to approach the client from a 'departmental' view, concerned more with the problems posed for the organisation than with the problems faced by the client. When the services offered by the department do not fit the needs of a particular client, those needs are reinterpreted so that they do fit. Where an adequate range of alternatives is not available, for example in education and accommodation, this is a real threat. Professionals must be protected from these pressures. One way to achieve this may be to devolve authority to small teams that are directly responsible for the delivery of services. Mittler (1979) discussed several pieces of research which indicated that: 'direct care staff develop resident-orientated as opposed to institution-orientated care in direct proportion to the extent that they themselves are given responsibility for decision making.' Such 'patch-based services' could provide a pattern for the future (see chapter four).

The problem of time

The use of time for organisational activities instead of for direct contact with clients is only one aspect of the problem. A larger part of the problem concerns the sheer volume of work thrust on most professionals and their inability for rational control. This also creates a pressure to 'get on with the job' when they do meet clients. Each different professional will narrow their focus down in different ways and none may have the time to establish the kind of broad relationship necessary to see the client's life in the round as they themselves see it.

One possible way out of this dilemma is the establishment of a key-worker or 'named person' system (DES, 1975). A single worker is designated by the team as the key-worker for one person or family. Ideally the client should be involved in this choice, because they need to get on well with whoever is appointed (Anderson, 1982). With each professional as a key-worker to a small number of clients, more time is available to build up good relationships. With key-workers, individualised planning may occur providing a coherent structure for the whole service system.

For this system to operate, those professionals who are not key-workers for a particular client will have to cede considerable responsibility or authority to their colleagues. This is possible only if there is already much trust and co-operation. In turn, the key-workers may need to expand their skills and change some of their usual ways of working (Cameron, 1985; Le Poidevin, 1985). This may be difficult for some professionals (Bowling, 1981).

Client inhibition

Professionals are powerful (Robinson, 1978; Wilding, 1982). They may not always feel this, but from the client's view they do control many important rewards and sanctions. In contrast, the client usually has little direct power to exert over the professional. This can affect what clients reveal about themselves. Edgerton (1979), in an intensive study of ex-hospital residents, noted how his fellow research workers 'often witnessed highly compelling performances in which ... a retarded person succeeds in convincing his or her social worker that some outrageous lie is the absolute truth'.

The problem is exacerbated when professionals are surrounded by a social mystique which they elaborate for themselves (Horobin, 1983). For example, jargon and shorthand are used in ways which make the client feel less competent; staff wear uniforms or arrange their offices to indicate their power and special status. Even when staff visit the client's own home, their self-confidence may contrast with uncertainty felt by the client. The way in which professionals conduct the encounter is also likely to spell out clearly what they see as relevant and important. The effect of all this may be to make clients passive, even when they are given the opportunity to contribute.

This problem can only be tackled by changing the balance of power in the relationship. Wright and Haycox outline an interesting proposal for allocating a care budget to each client (see chapter seven). This would be controlled by the client or the guardian and used to purchase the services that they felt were needed. This proposal would have the effect of making most professionals dependent on their clients. In addition, clients might be helped to deal better with professionals. One experiment has offered assertiveness training to parents of children with a mental handicap (Firth, 1986). Parent workshops on home teaching can have a similar effect in making parents more confident and competent in their subsequent dealings with professionals (Cunningham, 1983). It may also be possible to make the 'dramatic structuring' of encounters between clients and professionals less inhibiting. The important factor is how these encounters look to clients, rather than how they are seen by professionals (Pugh and Russell, 1977).

Burnout

Work in human services often involves considerable uncertainty and conflict, particularly where staff have established open relationships with their clients. This has only recently been acknowledged. Consequently staff have found it difficult to talk openly about their feelings and were offered little support. Staff have used a range of defences which have distanced them from their clients. For example, staff have withdrawn into technical preoccupations or focused on clients' behaviour to the exclusion of their subjective perceptions and feelings; they may have felt apathy, cynicism and irritation with clients for making life difficult. In places, these responses became collective and new idealistic entrants to the workplace were rapidly socialised into these largely defensive approaches to work. Sometimes this expressed itself in a negative and defensive trade unionism (Cherniss, 1980; Edelwich and Brodsky, 1980; Simpkin, 1984; Zastrow, 1983). As yet the difficulties have rarely been confronted systematically in mental handicap, but there are an increasing number of references to it in the literature (Anderson, 1982; Owens and Birchenall, 1979; Sang, 1984).

The problem can occur on several levels. First, it can arise in openly confronting the pain, distress and uncertainty which many clients face in their lives. Second, professionals often find themselves trapped between clients' needs and desires, and what organisations can or are prepared to offer. Third, organisations themselves often expose their employees to excessive pressures, conflicting demands and uncertainties. For example, the demands made on them may exceed their resources for coping effectively, or they may not have been given either clear goals or meaningful feedback on how they are progressing. This inhibits the establishment of good relationships with clients.

The problems are complex and need to be tackled from a variety of angles. One of the central themes involves the development of better support structures. Traditionally, where such structures have existed, they have been part of the process of supervision of employees by a more senior employee. These do have their place, but they involve two fundamental weaknesses. First, they can leave the supervisor in a very exposed situation, expected to help those they are supervising but with no one to turn to themselves and feeling unable to reveal 'weakness' to their subordinates. Second, in combining supervision and management with support, there is a real danger that those being supervised will be reluctant to reveal to their superiors what might be seen as 'failings'. There is a need to develop more egalitarian, horizontal support structures where, if senior staff are included, they are treated as equal participants and expected to share their own difficulties (Cassee, 1975). Alternatively, outside 'consultants' can be used, thus divorcing the support function entirely from the organisational structure. Either way, an ethos needs to be cultivated where distress, uncertainty and doubt can be expressed and shared.

Partnership

Traditionally, relationships between professionals and their clients have been one-sided, dominated by the 'expert' who determined what was needed. This was encouraged by the professional emphasis on the need for detachment and objectivity, if the client's problem was to be rationally and effectively resolved. Clients were stereotyped as ignorant, irrational, fragile and emotionally unstable (Mathey and Vernick, 1975; Roth, 1974). People with a mental handicap rarely entered the discussion. These negative views of the client were used to justify the one-sided relationships.

There has been a growing interest recently in a more active role for clients and a reconsideration of the role of the professional. The term 'partnership' has frequently been used to summarise these changes although it has been used to cover a wide variety of practices (Mittler, 1983). Significantly, there has been little discussion of client dominance as opposed to partnership. There is no solution which will be perfect for every person. Some clients will find it difficult to enter into a genuine partnership at times of crisis or where there is an emotional block. Equally, there will be times when the client may appropriately take the dominant role in a partnership (Pugh and Russell, 1977; Wright, 1960). More discussion is required to determine which circumstances should lead to different types of professional-client relationship (Freidson, 1970).

Clients' rights

The literature on partnership (Daly, *et al.*, 1985; Mittler and McConachie, 1983a; Pugh, 1981; Pugh and Russell, 1977; Turnbull and Winton, 1984) reflects diverse interests and reveals a variety of reasons for favouring the idea. There has been increasing opposition to the way in which professionals and services intrude in people's lives. This has been called the revolt of the client (Haug and Sussman, 1969; Lopata, 1976) and has been reflected in the growth of vocal parent pressure-groups and in a self-advocacy movement amongst people with a mental handicap. The literature has also begun to show a shift in emphasis. McCloskey (1980), for example, has noted a movement towards a recognition of the rights of people with a mental handicap as outlined in the United Nations Declaration of Rights of the Mentally Handicapped. These changes are reflected in legalisation. For example, American laws have enforced parents' right to a substantial say in their child's education (Turnbull and Winton, 1984) and the 1981 Education Act in Britain has given parents new, if rather weaker rights in this area (Mittler, 1983). After the heavy-handed paternalism which they have so often faced in the past, clients have a right as citizens and human beings to have a major say in decisions that directly affect their lives.

Quality of services

Traditionally, services were designed by professionals who decided what the client needed. In a survey of the family care of children with a severe mental handicap, Wilkin (1977) noted this could lead to major discrepancies between what mothers felt was necessary and what was provided. There may be occasions when a professional is justified in concluding that what a client feels they want is different from what they really need. However, this argument needs justification each time it is used. Where there is a large discrepancy, the quality of the service is open to question.

People with a mental handicap and their families know their own lives, and what is important to them, in a different way to professional understanding. Clients need more opportunity to be understood and to be given more information so that they can make an informed choice about their pattern of service provision (Mathey and Vernick, 1975). For example, a report of the Social Work Service Development Group (1984) noted a variety of ways of supporting informal carers and emphasized the rights of such carers to choose the model of care best suited to their own needs. It pointed out the importance of partnership between professionals, volunteers and informal carers in achieving this.

Effectiveness of services

A third argument for partnership has been concerned with how to make services more effective. Although this literature has been mainly concerned with the importance of partnership with parents, wherever possible partnership with people with a mental handicap should also be established (Firth, 1986; Mittler and McConachie, 1983b; Newson, 1981; Pugh and Russell, 1977; Turnbull and Winton, 1984).

Services for people with a mental handicap are concerned with helping and supporting people and not with repairing 'defective machines'. Machines do not have opinions, feelings, views or self-knowledge which can affect the success of work. Their motivation is not important. Human beings are different, consequently it is necessary to work *with* them rather than just for them.

Clients need to identify with the goals set and the means chosen to achieve these goals. The programmes that physiotherapists, speech therapists or psychologists develop for clients may be eminently sensible from a professional viewpoint, but they are liable to collapse if they do not take account of the wider context of the family. To avoid this, parents need to talk openly, as well as to listen and answer questions. The professional needs to give information, as well as receive it.

Where the situation involves a person with a mental handicap who lives at home, partnership with parents becomes vital as the family will be the most important single influence on his or her development. Daly *et al.* (1985) described any service which does not actively involve parents as 'firing on only one cylinder'. In most cases, the child's closest relationship will be with its parents, and the parents' views very likely will affect the child's motivation. Children spend more time with their parents than with any professional, particularly in the early years. They simply have more learning time there than anywhere else. Further, unless behaviours which have first been learned in a professional setting (e.g. school or clinic) are reinforced and generalised in the home setting, they will be of only limited value to the child. Parents develop an extensive knowledge of their own children and how they behave in a variety of settings. They also develop unique ways of handling them. Collins and Collins (1974) conveyed this by talking about parents as 'twenty-four hour professionals'. Their knowledge often will be un-structured and the ways of dealing with the child will be insufficiently focused and sometimes unsuccessful. In a partnership with profes-sionals, parents can have far more positive impact on the child's development. The danger is that professionals may still see the purpose of involving parents narrowly as a way of improving the child's functioning rather than also in terms of the rights or needs of the parents (Turnbull and Winton, 1984). Again this reflects a one-sided view of partnerships.

The cost of services

Professional time is very costly. A number of writers have suggested that partnership with parents is important because it is a particularly cost-effective way of extending services (Pugh and Russell, 1977; Turn-bull and Winton, 1984). Parents can provide low-cost and continuous care for their child. This is a perfectly valid argument, but it highlights the danger that partnerships might be abused for economic reasons.

Two models of partnership with parents

Summaries of experiments in partnership indicate how much diversity exists (Daly *et al.*, 1985; Mittler and McConachie, 1983b; Pugh and Russell, 1977). Certainly no single model dominates the field. Mittler (1983) identifies two broad approaches. The first involves the parent as co-teacher or co-therapist with the professional. A more accurate description might be that the parent is a valuable aide or assistant. In this model, the professional retains considerable control in the relationship, with the parent acting as an aide or assistant. The professional primarily has determined the goals and methods, with his or her professional expertise. The parent has co-operated in the professional's plan. For example, Gardner (1983) described a home–school partnership and argued that parents often experience problems in choosing appropriate tasks to teach the child. She suggested that this need not present a problem if the school operates a structured curriculum in which teachers select appropriate behavioural targets for each child. Parents 'can then assist school staff by sharing the teaching of the weekly targets or by assisting in the generalisation process through teaching targets already learned at school under the different conditions at home' (Gardner, 1983).

Subsequent involvement of parents with teachers in selecting the next target does little to lessen the overall tone of professional dominance. Even this fairly limited shift in relationships, however, can boost parental self-esteem and counter the corrosive effects of their feelings of helplessness and failure.

The second model has been described by Mittler as the consumer model (Mittler, 1983). This involves a shift in the professional's role from that of clinician to consultant. Here the professional shares his or her knowledge, skills and expertise with the parents. The parents then choose from this information according to their own needs and life-styles. This model gives parents an opportunity to grasp the principles and not just learn a recipe for an effective intervention (Russell, 1985). The discussion progresses beyond the ideal of equal partnership towards a measure of client dominance: 'a two-way process of joint assessment and decision making ... in which each side has areas of knowledge and skill that it contributes to the joint task of working with the child' (Mittler, 1983).

This approach suggests that professionals have much to learn from parents. Cunningham and Jeffree (1977) have described how parents contributed knowledge to their parent workshops which proved useful, both to other parents and to themselves as tutors. Mittler also argued that professionals and parents should share their feelings and help each other during difficult periods when there is little progress. This is a very different model of both partnership and the professional's role. Which-ever method of partnership is proposed there remain several unresolved problems.

Problems with partnership

Pressure on parents

Parents who have a child with a mental handicap already are likely to be under more pressure than other parents. This is something which has now been recognised, with the parents' right of access to respite care properly acknowledged (Social Work Service Development Group, 1984). It is ironic that at the same time they have been encouraged to adopt a substantial new responsibility with respect to their child's development. The costs of this may well be outweighed by the gain from more active involvement but this will require careful monitoring.

It is not simply that more involvement will use precious time which could be used to meet other needs. It also places a considerable moral responsibility on parents. If their child does not progress as had been hoped or if they do not give as much time to working with him or her as they felt they should have done, then they are likely to feel guilty. Buckley (1985), in a small study of parents with a child with Down's syndrome, suggested that this was quite common, even in the case of those in favour of such home teaching. Parents may also find they have changed role as parent in undesirable ways. This danger was illustrated by the following comment from a physically disabled woman looking back on her own childhood: 'Something happens in a parent when relating to his disabled child. He forgets that they're a kid first .... I would be off in a euphoric state drawing or colouring or cutting out paper dolls and as often as not the activity would be turned into an occupational therapy session .... That era ended when I finally let loose a long and exhausting tirade. "I'm just a kid, you can't therapise me all the time .... I don't think about my handicap all the time like you do!"' (Turnbull and Winton, 1984).

Some of these problems could be avoided if the consumer model of partnership was adopted. In this model the form and extent of a particular parent's involvement would be flexibly negotiated, taking account of the family's wider needs and concerns. Such a model explicitly acknowledges the parent's right to opt out of partnership. Not all professionals take such a parent-orientated stance. For example, Gardner (1983) stated that: 'While many parents could, under optimum conditions, exhibit proficient teaching skills, we also discovered that parents were not teaching their children either long enough or often enough .... The problem seemed to stem not from a lack of enthusiasm but lack of direction'. Such a view can lead to pressure on parents which does not take adequate account of their broader needs. It would be better if such pressure could be reduced or avoided.

Disagreement

Curiously, there is virtually no discussion of what happens when parents and professionals disagree. The assumption seems to be that they will always reach an amicable and negotiated agreement. If this is true, then this area of human life must be unique! Equally, there is little discussion of whether there are occasions when the professional is justified in acting in secret, without prior consultation with the parents. Are there ever occasions when the professional is justified in withholding information from the parent, and in acting on their view of the child's needs even if this conflicts with that of the parents?

Practice

What really occurs in a partnership? There is a dearth of evidence on this question. Most of the information concerns demonstration projects which may well be atypical (Mittler, 1983). There are several reasons for concern about this scarcity of evidence. First, there is insufficient training of professionals to prepare them for a partnership role and, as a consequence, there is no reason to expect they will all adjust to being equal partners. Most will opt for something nearer the 'assistant' than the 'consumer' model of partnership. Turnbull and Turnbull (1982) have referred to several studies in the USA which suggested that teachers monopolise conversation with parents, with the parents' contributions largely confined to personal and family matters. Turnbull and Winton (1984), in a further study, suggested that many professionals preferred parents to have a more passive role and saw the main purpose of parental involvement as improving the child's functioning rather than a matter of parental rights. The pattern may be very different in Britain but the evidence is inconclusive.

In addition to the sources of power already discussed, professionals often have greater verbal fluency and persuasiveness than many parents. This is enhanced by the mystique which surrounds professionals in society. The consequence is that even when professionals think they are treating parents as equal partners, they may be controlling the encounters. Frank (1959) showed in his study of psychotherapy that even supposedly non-directive therapy is often highly directive. These doubts should not be taken as grounds for discounting or rejecting partnership. There is no doubt about its potential benefits. Many parents appreciate it, despite the additional demands it creates.

Partnership with people with a mental handicap

You don't like to be domineered too often; we're not kids, we're over twenty-one, we're not stupid. We don't like to be domineered .... If I didn't speak for myself I wouldn't be where I am today; I used to be shy, people just trod on your toes. I don't like to be domineered too much. It's not right. (CMH, 1973a)

Parents have always had a voice even if, until recently, much of what they said was subsequently reinterpreted by professionals. People with a mental handicap, however, often have no voice at all. This is now changing. There is an acknowledgement of adulthood and of the fact that people with a mental handicap should have a substantial say, if not a controlling voice, in all their services. Central to this is an emphasis on their rights and on the importance of ensuring that they have real choices in life. If this is to be achieved, professionals need to view their relationships with people with a mental handicap much more in terms of a partnership than at present. It is clear 'that staff and parents frequently and massively underestimate the abilities even of mentally handicapped people whom they know well' (Mittler, 1983). There are also limits, and 'it is important not to lose sight of the severe disabilities of mentally handicapped people in our enthusiasm to stress their more positive achievements' (Mittler, 1979). The problem is that we do not know quite what is realistic and what is not; the opinion of the person with a mental handicap is crucial.

Many people with a mental handicap need both encouragement and help to enable them to exercise their rights and make effective choices. Sometimes the need for such support will diminish, but for many the need will remain substantial. The resulting problems cannot be resolved simply by emphasising the adult status of people with a mental handicap. These problems include the need to establish an accurate understanding of the person's feelings; to offer them real choices; to address their real vulnerability; and to clarify the role of parents.

Accurate understanding

If other people are to play an important role in enabling people with a mental handicap to exercise their rights and make choices, they need to establish an accurate understanding of how people see things and how they feel. This involves learning to encourage the person with a mental handicap to talk and then to listen openly without constant interruptions. In one conference set up to achieve this end it became clear that 'many people with a mental handicap have a background of experiences stretching back many years that they need to describe as part of their expression of views on changes they would like in their circumstances .... The non-handicapped people at the conference found it difficult to listen to these accounts with tolerance and genuine interest' (CMH, 1973b). Additionally, many people with a mental handicap have more reason than most for being wary about what they reveal of themselves because of the stigma that attaches to the label 'mental handicap' in our society and the power of other people in their lives (Edgerton, 1967; 1979).

Where the person has a severe disability, which seriously affects their ability to communicate verbally, there are multiple problems of accurate understanding. Anderson (1982) noted the need to find the meaning in their behaviour if we are not to treat them as 'cabbages' (*sic*), yet to do that may require substantial guesswork and an ability to imagine what their world feels like. The danger is that, in our need to make sense of them, we may impose our own incorrect meanings on them. Regardless of the degree of handicap, relationships require time, patience and humility; few professionals have all three. This demonstrates the importance of a 'key-worker' system and the need to listen carefully to others who spend more time with the person, such as parents, volunteers or advocates. None of this can, however, guarantee that the individual's real views and feelings will be stated.

The problem of effective choice

Many people with a mental handicap are able to express their thoughts and feelings and many have no problem about making real choices. Their problem is simply enacting their choices. Others face greater problems. For example, some people's experiences of the world may have been so impoverished that they find it difficult to conceive of alternatives. Considerable imagination is required to ensure that they can make meaningful choices. More is required than just asking them questions (Mittler, 1979). They need to be offered alternatives, shown a range of options and offered the chance to try them out. Only then can they make an informed choice. To help in this process, research workers have attempted to develop standard instruments which will help people with a mental handicap to express preferences in key areas of their lives (Mittler, 1983a). Even people with a severe handicap can generally express some reactions although their ways of doing so may be barely perceptible. Choices are also sometimes more apparent than real. For example, when hospital residents are consulted about where they want to live, they may, in practice, be prevented from choosing to stay in hospital. Administrative decisions may have already been made to close the hospital.

The problem of vulnerability

People with a mental handicap may be more vulnerable than others. First, the main concern of parents is their vulnerability to abuse, exploitation, danger, rejection and loneliness (Rescare, 1985). In modern society those risks are real. There are many steps that can and should be taken to make society more tolerant and accepting, but these lie largely in the future. Second, Wolfensberger (1972) has suggested that many adults with a mental handicap have weak self-images and feelings of insecurity. This makes them even more vulnerable to the dangers outlined above. Third, it has been suggested that people with a mental handicap 'are especially vulnerable to neglect of all kinds, especially educational neglect .... They are often less competent than others in learning incidentally, and in observing and imitating others, and many of them are also poorly endowed with "natural" curiosity to experiment and explore their environment' (Mittler, 1979).

The ability of many people with a mental handicap to cope with these problems may have been underestimated but not all their vulnerability can be made to disappear, however. Society has a complex responsibility to someone who is both an adult and who is also substantially more vulnerable than other people. The problem cannot be solved either by concentrating on the person's vulnerability, to the extent of over-protection, or by concentrating on their adult status and making no provision for protection or direction. Normalisation advocates in particular have found it difficult to adequately address these issues, perhaps because of their concern to stress the rights of people with a mental handicap as citizens, adults and human beings.

In practice elements of benevolent paternalism are apparent in many projects irrespective of their underlying philosophy. Given the vulnerability, the learning difficulties and the restricted experiences of particular individuals, some tempering of our commitment to equal rights, full choice and full partnership would sometimes seem justified. However, such paternalism must always be treated as the exception which needs justifying in each particular case and should be kept to the minimum. This means that it has to be openly acknowledged so that it is open to challenge. The difficulty is that paternalism is such a dirty word that people are reluctant to acknowledge it and often seek to gloss over and obscure its presence. Relationships must rest on a greater openness if any sort of partnership is to be established. This is possible to some extent even with people who are severely disabled.

The role of parents

Where people with a mental handicap are not more vulnerable than other people, there is no reason why the role of their parents should be any different from that of other parents of adult children. However, that may not be the case. Further, de facto, many parents are left to care for their adult son or daughter and do continue to make many decisions about their lives. There is a tripartite relationship involving the parent as well as the professional and the person with a mental handicap themselves. This reality cannot be ignored, even if there are no clear answers about how such a partnership should work or about how disputes should be resolved. Parents should not and, in practice, cannot be left on the sidelines.

Unfortunately, it is clear that that is precisely where many parents feel they have been placed and they are not happy about this (Rescare, 1985). Even sympathetic professionals have sometimes been guilty of encouraging this feeling. For example, Heron and Myers (1983) implicitly assume that professionals are always right about things like the risks which people should be encouraged to take. Parents have a role but it is to be encouraged, supported, persuaded so that they can live with the consequences of the professional's view. The challenge is to develop a structure of tripartite relationships which excludes neither the parent nor the person with a mental handicap. The challenge, though, cannot be evaded much longer because a number of recent developments are making the voice of both parents and people with a mental handicap themselves much more prominent in the debate.

The client's perspective

Self-help groups

One of the most notable developments in the welfare system since the last war has been the rapid growth of self-help groups (Killilea, 1974; Loney, 1981). In mental handicap, MENCAP (the Royal Society for Mentally Handicapped People) has dominated these developments. Self-help groups have acquired a romantic reputation. The reality is that they are generally very fragile (Richardson and Goodman, 1983). Few members are prepared to be really active and they have their own problems to cope with as well. None the less, groups can play an important role in parents' lives. They offer empathic, mutual support from others who have had similar experiences. They can offer successful role models, coping strategies and the opportunity to share and help. They provide valuable information, including how to deal with services and professionals, as well as support and encouragement to parents who want to become more active towards those services. By affecting parents' self-esteem, confidence and knowledge, they can have considerable effect on their relationships with professionals. This is often enhanced by the impact of MENCAP, locally and nationally, in asserting the parents' voice in their dealings with professionals and service providers. Some work has looked at how such groups can be supported and enabled by professionals (Richardson, 1984).

Self-advocacy

Parents have gained an increasingly powerful voice. Until recently, however, few people seriously considered the possibility that people with a mental handicap might speak up for themselves. An important development has been the growth of the National People First Movement (Williams and Shoultz, 1982). By 1979, one-sixth of the delegates at the annual conference of the Canadian Association of the Mentally Retarded were people with a mental handicap. Many of the local groups developed a strong and effective voice, speaking out, on behalf of people with a mental handicap, to professionals, parents, the media and thc legislature. Members have also supported and encouraged each other to stand up for their rights. Through membership of such groups, many people have gained in confidence and self-respect. However, few of the groups have been able to exist without an outside helper or adviser, and most have needed a period of preparation and training. The role of the adviser should be confined to a delicate, facilitative function in which help is offered only when it is required. This role requires further investigations. Developments in Britain are at a very early stage, and may reflect the fact that rights for people with a mental handicap are less established in law in Britain. Britain is also a more paternalistic society.

Citizen advocacy

Citizen advocacy developed in North America in the early 1970s in respect of the need for people with a mental handicap to be represented by a non-professional advocate. It involves 'a private citizen entering into a relationship with and representing the interests of a mentally handicapped person who needs assistance to improve his or her quality of life and obtain full rights and entitlements' (Sang, 1985). It depends on the creation of local independent advocacy offices which recruit, select and train lay advocates so they can be matched with a person with a mental handicap who needs and wants such a service. The advocate's prime commitment is to his or her protégé and the relationship is expected to be long-term. The advocate's role may be very extensive (Sang, 1985; Wolfensberger, 1983). It can encompass anything from friendship and emotional support, to providing practical help in every-day living, to helping people obtain benefits, to co-operating in indivi-dual treatment programmes and intervening in instances of abuse or neglect. The advocate should also encourage the maximum possible independence in his or her protégé, including development of skills to speak for themselves more effectively.

In the USA, citizen advocacy has been powerfully supported by a parallel, legal advocacy movement, concerned specifically with defending the legal rights of people with a mental handicap. In Britain, however, where these rights have been made less specific in law, the fledgeling advocacy movement has been much more dependent on the co-operation of existing agencies. This risks that the independence of the movement will be compromised. There have been few truly indepen-dent studies of citizen advocacy, and none has included direct in-formation of what occurs between advocate and protégé (Kurtz, 1975).

This is a serious deficiency, given the complex and ambiguous role allocated to the advocate. Further, it is unclear how their introduction affects the complicated relationships between the professionals, parents and people with a mental handicap. None the less, the movement has a potentially important role to play in strengthening the voice of people with a mental handicap.

Conclusion

This chapter has raised far more questions than it has been able to answer and posed more problems than it has been able to solve. Relationships, though, remain at the heart of things. Only if people can further improve these, by opening up communication, improving mutual understanding and developing a sense of partnership will people be able to avoid going down still more wrong turnings. This is a difficult and uncertain challenge but an exciting one. The first stage in this journey must be to confront some of the difficulties people may face on the way.

Chapter six

Normalisation or 'social role valorization': an adequate philosophy?

Michael Bayley

Difficulties can arise over the understanding of 'normalisation' and the danger exists that normalisation may represent a lifestyle which is valued by its exponents, rather than by people with a mental handicap themselves. Other authors have noted this (Wolfensberger, 1983). This chapter explores the same issue but from a different perspective.

The whole normalisation movement should be seen against the background of 'abnormalisation', which was the daily experience of many people with a mental handicap at the time when the movement began. Against such a background, especially the regimes in some of the larger 'subnormality' hospitals, it made very good sense to ask the question: 'What is normal?' It was also a very powerful way of helping persons working with people with a mental handicap to see how distorted some of their perceptions and expectations had become. Nirje (1973) emphasised the importance of a normal pattern of daily, weekly and yearly routines, and indicated the basic level at which these questions needed to be asked. It is relevant to continue asking these questions. Problems, originally evident in large hospitals for people with a mental handicap, have been transferred to smaller units, such as local authority hostels.

The debate has moved on and is now focused on the adequacy of the notion of 'normality'. This has been reflected in the writing of Wolfensberger who has adopted the notion of 'culturally valued roles', and recognised the importance of the culture within which the person with a mental handicap is living. The focus, however, remains very clearly on the concept of developing valued social roles for people with a mental handicap. The expression 'social role valorization' was suggested to overcome misunderstandings (Wolfensberger, 1983). The ultimate goal of this approach was defined as 'enhancement of the social role of persons or groups at risk of social devaluation.' This could be achieved by two major sub-goals: 'enhancement of their social image' and 'enhancement of perceived competencies'.

This approach has focused explicitly on the roles of people with handicaps:

> It is important to distinguish between the valorization of the role of the person, and the valuing (or valorization) of the person him/herself. When we speak of valuing the person, we step at least partially outside a theoretical framework that is profoundly anchored to empiricism and into the realm of super-empirical value systems. (Wolfensberger, 1983)

This position, however, has a fundamental flaw. It has trapped the whole debate within the framework of the given culture. What is 'normal' or 'valued' within a particular culture may be open to serious question. The limitations of this stance are clear in the way 'enhancement of the social role of persons at risk of social devaluation' has been described as the ultimate goal. It may well be that individualistic achievement or success-orientated societal values, which emphasise people's independence rather than their interdependence, are profoundly unhelpful to people with a mental handicap (and many other people). Instead, the focus should be on valuing the person; this makes it possible to question not just any undervalued social roles experienced by people with a mental handicap, but also the values that society holds which appear to deny such people the opportunity to develop in the way which is best for them. This has been noted elsewhere:

> We have seen in the field of mental handicap how much the spirit of reform, both past and present, is tied to the promise that mentally handicapped people can be improved – through changing they become more acceptable. Again and again this path to greater acceptance is seen as though some kind of normality. (Ryan and Thomas, 1980)

The authors go on to say that the main exceptions are the 'various religious, spiritual and alternative communities most of whom have a philosophy of accepting mentally handicapped people as they are.' Such communities also 'have a strong appreciation of what mentally handicapped people can give to others'. In contrast, Wolfensberger has argued:

Such orientation often results in a defiant challenge to 'the world' to similarly value the person regardless of the person's identity and characteristics. That such an appeal has merit and validity I do not question, but I do assert that it is almost totally ineffective in bringing about the desired goal. (Wolfensberger, 1983)

The work of organisations such as *L'Arche* in France must question such a sweeping statement. It is paradoxical that it has been assumed that valuing people with a mental handicap for themselves is incompatible with working to develop socially valued roles for them. An organisation like *L'Arche* puts a major question mark against whether roles valued by a particular society are necessarily appropriate for people with a mental handicap.

We ... have to allow for the possibility that mentally handicapped people may wish to question and reject some of the more exploitative and oppressive standards of our society, just as many non-handicapped people do. Many people choose to live in various unconventional ways, for example, in communes in the country, or shared households in the city, to reject certain standards of conventional dress and typical sex-role behaviour, and mentally handicapped people may wish to do so too. (Ryan and Thomas, 1980)

But an attitude which positively values people with a mental handicap for themselves goes beyond this. Referring to the work of Thomas Weihs, a follower of Rudolph Steiner and one of the founders of the Camphill movement, and Jean Vanier, founder of *L'Arche* community, Ryan and Thomas comment:

These writings are much more than an invitation to take pity on the suffering; they are also a challenge to see what mentally handicapped people reveal about ourselves and the kind of society we live in. It is not just fanciful romanticization to claim that mentally handicapped people can be an inspiration to others, an indictment of the inhuman values of the rest of the world, a reminder of the buried and more vulnerable parts of ourselves. These perceptions are of decisive importance in allowing us to value them, in finding some common humanity. (Ryan and Thomas, 1980)

If there is something important to be learnt from bodies such as *L'Arche* about the fundamental assumptions about people with a mental handicap, then it is necessary to understand those assumptions.

L'Arche and its philosophy

A single term to encapsulate the distinctive approach of *L'Arche* to people with a mental handicap might be 'unconditional acceptance'. This means that the person with a mental handicap is accepted unconditionally because they are valued as people in their own right, and not because of anything they might be able to do or of any ways in which they might improve.

L'Arche is an explicitly Christian organisation. The theological rationale for its approach is that as God in Christ loves and has accepted all of us unconditionally, sinners as we are, so are we bound to show the same love and unconditional acceptance to other people as they are. They are all, like us, people for whom Christ died, including people with a mental handicap. It follows that we are all, whether handicapped or not, equally in need of, and dependent on, God's love and mercy. God has accepted all of us as we are without demanding that we become better people before he will accept us. One does not have to earn God's acceptance; all that is required of us is to acknowledge that we are accepted by him.

This view relates to the central Christian belief that what God in his love offers to people is 'unconditional acceptance'. This has always been a difficult concept for men and women to accept, especially when they have been conditioned into a moralistic way of thinking, and believe that they have to earn the right to be accepted by God. The belief that God offers unconditional acceptance to all men and women is the dynamic which lies behind the approach of *L'Arche*. This understanding of what God, in Christ, has done for people reduces to insignificance whether or not people have a handicap. The overwhelming belief that, whether handicapped or not, all people are brothers and sisters in Christ, is what makes the sense of a common humanity such a powerful force in *L'Arche*. It is this strong belief in a common humanity which enables *L'Arche* to welcome people as helpers, whether they call themselves Christians or not.

It has been important to emphasise the belief in a common humanity, based on God's unconditional acceptance of all people, because so long as this is recognised, it removes the danger of condescension. People with a mental handicap are not objects of charity but, first and foremost, individual people, like all other people who are valued and accepted by God. The charter of the Communities of *L'Arche* states: 'We believe that each person, whether handicapped or not, has a unique and mysterious value. The handicapped person is a complete human being and as such he (*sic*) has the right to life, to care, to education and work' (Vanier, 1976).

In addition, there is in the Christian gospel a particular duty placed on Christians to concern themselves with the poor, the homeless and the outcasts of society. The parable of the sheep and the goats is the starkest statement of that duty.

> When the Son of Man comes in His glory . . . before him will be gathered all the nations, and He will separate them one from another as a shepherd separates his sheep from the goats, and He will place the sheep at His right hand, but the goats at the left. Then the King will say to those at His right hand, 'Come O blessed of my Father, inherit the kingdom prepared for you from the foundation of the world; for I was hungry and you gave me food, I was thirsty and you gave me drink, I was a stranger and you welcomed me, I was naked and you clothed me, I was sick and you visited me, I was in prison and you came to me'. Then the righteous will answer Him, 'Lord, when did we see thee hungry and feed thee, or thirsty and give thee drink? And when did we see thee a stranger and welcome thee, or naked and clothe thee? And when did we see thee sick or in prison and visit thee?' And the King will answer them, 'Truly, I say to you, as you did it to one of the least of my brethren, you did it to me'. Then He will say to those at his left hand, 'Depart from me, you cursed, into the eternal fire prepared for the devil and his angels; for I was thirsty and you gave me no drink, I was a stranger and you did not welcome me, naked and you did not clothe me, sick and in prison and you did not visit me'. Then they will answer, 'Lord when did we see thee hungry or thirsty or a stranger or naked or sick or in prison, and did not minister to thee?' Then He will answer them, 'Truly, I say to you, as you did it not to one of the least of these, you did it not to me'. And they will go away into eternal punishment, but the righteous into eternal life. (Matthew 25, verses 31-46)

The identification of poor people and people in need with Christ himself has always been a powerful force behind various forms of Christian social and charitable action. Such an identification, along with the clear understanding of our common humanity, are needed to prevent concern from becoming patronising. This is expressed in the statement of Communities of *L'Arche*:

Our anxiety is great, faced with the world of suffering and the numbers of mentally handicapped people who are rejected, without work, without homes or who are shut up in psychiatric hospitals. But this anxiety must not paralyse us. On the contrary it should incite us to work for those who are rejected by creating communities of peace and also to labour that our society develop a greater sense of justice and brotherly (*sic*) concern toward all men (*sic*).

The evidence of *L'Arche* and similar organisations suggests the benefits of a positive valuing of people with a mental handicap. Their approach involves not the stoic acceptance of a burden, but a positive valuing of people with a mental handicap, both for gifts they bring and for what they can teach us.

Handicapped people, particularly those who are less able, are frequently endowed with qualities of heart which serve to remind so-called normal people that their own hearts are closed. Their simplicity frequently serves to reveal our own duplicity, untruthfulness, and hypocrisy. Their acceptance of their own situation and their humility frequently reveals our pride and our refusal to accept others as they are. So-called normal people often have interior barriers that prevent them from relating with others in a simple way. All of us have deep needs to love and be loved. All of us are in the conflict of our own fear of death and of our own poverty. We so quickly pretend that we are more clever, more intelligent, and more powerful than we actually are. So often we flee reality by throwing ourselves into activity, culture, the struggle for power and prestige. We lose contact with our deep inner selves. Handicapped people do not always have these barriers. In their poverty they are more simple and loving and thus reveal to us the poverty of our riches. (Vanier, 1976)

This attitude has been illustrated by Hazel West:

The busker stamped and blew and knocked and flapped, setting all his one-man band instruments vibrating and jangling, his colourful clothing adding to the sense of joy and abandon set by his music. Many shoppers had paused, dumped their sagging bags in a wide circle around him, and rested from the concentrated preoccupation with their chores.

Suddenly, into the circle ran a slight girl, in trousers, anorak and woolly hat. In the centre she gave out a great roar of excitement, raised her arms high above her head and began to dance.

She danced from sheer joy which sprang spontaneously in response to the music, swaying her body, waving her arms, tapping and stepping, twisting her head now this way, now that, before the silent crowd. Soon she became conscious of her audience and with another excited roar, and a laughing command which might have been 'Come on', she approached people in the circle with both hands outstretched.

None was quite bold enough to join her in the centre, but some, surprised by her abandoned jubilation, and touched by her trusting invitation, smiled, took her offered hands for a few moments and swayed with her till she moved on to others around the circle.

As the tambourine man played on, she began to sing, not words, but in a jumble of nonsense syllables in rhythm, if not in tune, to the music. One or two of the crowd frowned and moved away at her approach, but undaunted she moved on and round, accepting any friendly response, and then moving back to the centre to continue her own dance.

She was of indeterminate age, not quite a child, but not an adult either, blue-eyed, fair with the distinctive features of people with Down's Syndrome. She was in fact aged twenty-two. And she was my daughter.

I watched this public exhibition with mixed and turbulent emotions. Confused by both guilt and pride, I hung at the back of the crowd, and looked around to gauge the response – and yes, I confess it, to see if anyone might recognise me.

Strange that we should so little value the traits of people like Lucy ... Perhaps they reflect facets of ourselves which are hidden, underdeveloped, undernourished. If that is so, then there is so much that we can learn from Lucy. Secretly, I confess it, I am proud to be her mother.

Lucy cannot talk at all and understands little verbal language. But her every smile and action communicate a clear message: Love me as I am – not for what you hope to turn me into. Respect me as I am – I merit your respect. (West, 1985)

A sense of joy and jubilation is experienced by people who visit the houses of *L'Arche*. There is a sense of celebration in people who, on the face of it, do not have much to celebrate. The assistants and people with a mental handicap always have meals together. These shared meals are an important part of the life of the houses and they provide the setting for much plain, straightforward fun. For example, Vanier tells how:

> When we've had oranges for dessert at *L'Arche*, we sometimes start chucking the peel about at the end of the meal. Everyone gets into it. An Englishman once asked me if this was a traditional French custom. I don't know about that! But I do know that it is one way to bring people out of their isolation to express themselves joyfully – especially if they can't communicate with words. People who cannot participate in interesting conversations can participate through play. When a piece of orange peel arrives on their nose, they are delighted – and they throw it back. (Vanier, 1979)

This may seem trivial, but it catches something of the sense of fun and joy. There is nothing superficial about that joy. It is not the joy which comes from pretending that nothing is wrong, or ignoring the existence of pain, grief and unhappiness:

> Visitors are often astonished at the joy they sense at *L'Arche*. Their impression surprises me, too, because I know how much suffering some people are carrying in our communities. I wonder if all joy doesn't somehow spring from suffering and sacrifice. (Vanier, 1979)

Perhaps this is the most distinctive contribution that *L'Arche* can make to the way in which we respond to people with a mental handicap. At the heart of the Christian gospel stands the crucifixion and resurrection of Christ. Christian people see this as the redeeming power of love triumphing over (and through) suffering and evil. In this way, suffering is not pushed to the edge but is seen as something that must be embraced, and overcome. But when people who suffer, poor people and those with a mental handicap are acknowledged and accepted in the name of Christ, and in the power of Christ, the result is that the community:

> becomes a place of reconciliation and forgiveness, where each person feels carried by others and carries them. It is a place of friendship among those who know they are weak but know too that they are loved and forgiven. Thus community is the place for celebration. (Vanier, 1979)

This section has tried to give some insight into the beliefs and motivation behind the approach of the various religious, spiritual or alternative communities. People in *L'Arche* would admit that there are always difficulties in working with the ideals in practice. Neither *L'Arche* nor other similar organisations claim to have a monopoly of love and unconditional acceptance of people with a mental handicap. They do, however, provide a focal point where the implications of that approach can be seen with clarity. The values that such organisations represent are not those of society. That is part of their value, but this has important policy implications.

Unconditional acceptance in an unaccepting society

There is an immediate problem with putting unconditional acceptance of people with a mental handicap into practice in a society which does not accept them unconditionally. In the past this problem has been resolved by withdrawal from the world. This is true of several alternative organisations, such as the Camphill Villages and other geographically isolated residential sites. But withdrawal from the world is not a criticism that can be applied across the board to all alternative communities. Town-based *L'Arche* communities, for example, do not suggest lack of commitment to helping people with a mental handicap to learn and develop more socially acceptable roles. However, the policy-maker inevitably encounters a tension; he or she is faced by the need to provide settings where people with a mental handicap will be accepted unconditionally and valued, but this may bring attendant problems of segregation. If the policy-maker decides to promote physical integration, this means that people with a mental handicap may only be accepted conditionally. Such conditional acceptance may bring many problems of inappropriate pressures.

This tension is always present. It is always difficult to decide how much to expose people with a mental handicap to risk by offering them opportunities of learning and developing. It is also important to create environments which both offer a degree of protection to some people with a mental handicap and provide opportunities to learn, develop and lead fulfilling lives for others. A major contribution of the alternative communities will continue to be living out the implications of unconditional acceptance of people with a mental handicap. It is artificial, however, to separate that from the subject of integration into mainstream society. Various alternative structures may make an important contribution to the debate. It would be a disaster for policy (and morally wrong) to maintain that integration and unconditional acceptance are incompatible in principle.

Normalisation and housing

Housing for people with a mental handicap illustrates problems that can occur when the principle of normalisation or 'social role valorization' is accepted as the ultimate goal. Those who adhere strictly to the principle of normalisation argue that housing for people with a mental handicap invariably should be in ordinary housing. One example of this is the so-called 'apartheid' thinking:

> Just as in racial apartheid ... there is protectiveness. 'It's for their own good!' Similar things were said of black slaves in the Deep South. In the world of handicap apartheid thus becomes an endeavour to create a world free from stress and challenge. (Tyne, 1985)

The dangers are very real, but in the 'apartheid' approach there is an element lacking which may be due to an inadequate frame of reference. According to normalisation, it is particular *roles* for people with a mental handicap that are valued, rather than the people themselves. It is unfortunate, however, that the way people behave often does not conform to their theoretical position. This is not to suggest that normalisation does not personally value people with a mental handicap. Indeed, the opposite is true. The problem is not at the personal level, but at the policy level. For example:

> As we go about the country [we see] ... health and local authorities continuing to run institutions, some of which they say will close. But their replacements in a great many places are mainly 'prettier' versions of the old – often now described as 'villages' .... At least people were embarrassed about the old institutions. The new institutions seem set to perpetuate exactly the same ways of life for people with handicaps. Now, though, this is not the result of sad neglect or lack of resources. At least some of the time, it's the result of systematic, purposeful, intellectually thought out oppression that is the expression of theories based on apartheid thinking. (Tyne, 1985)

There is much to support these criticisms but it is hard to align them with, for example, this description by Hazel West of where her daughter Lucy lives:

> Twenty years old, attractive, vivacious, the body of a woman and the mental age of two-and-a-half .... Friendly, fun-loving, gregarious, with little understanding of language or of the world, Lucy has been happy for some years now: cared for by concerned staff in a village-like community, though in fact a small DHSS hospital for about 80 or so. She has been extended by training in all the self-help skills; occupied with every possible activity that she can manage; been stimulated and stimulating; has revelled in her swimming and discos and drama; excelled at her riding; and was chosen to ride before Princess Anne at Hever Castle. She has worn down her speech therapists and Makaton teachers in their hardly successful attempts to teach her speech and language. She has remained, so far, buoyant and stable and ego-strong throughout all their attempts to stretch her. Obviously she's happy with herself as she is. She has been, and she knows it, a full contributing member of her own 'community'. But a policy decision means that Lucy must move and for two and a half years now two social services departments and I have been looking for an alternative. That she has been happy and fulfilled in her present community she amply demonstrates in her obvious *joie de vivre*. (West, 1985)

Should this account be written off because such an environment might prove too restrictive for someone who is more able? Is the obvious satisfaction Lucy derives from this setting to be ignored on the grounds that the roles she can play there are insufficiently valued by society? Is her way of life to be considered unacceptable because she is insufficiently integrated? It is not possible to answer these questions without knowing more. Such questions should, however, be asked, considered and answered. It is not sufficient to rule the questions out of order on the grounds that the setting does not conform to a policy of normalisation. To do so would be a clear example of the roles that people with a mental handicap play being valued more highly than the people themselves.

Is it, for example, more important for Lucy to behave in a quiet, unobtrusive way, adopting a role which is as close as possible to that of a 'normal' member of society, which will cause no embarrassment to anyone; or is it more important that she should be given the opportunity to develop her own potential as a person, and behave sometimes in the comic way described earlier, which may embarrass people with normal inhibitions? The danger of concentrating on roles is that individual people, in all their variety, are forgotten. Theory may be seen as more important than the people for whose benefit the theory was developed in the first place.

Other questions have been raised about what 'pattern of normality' is being employed. A description of how two children with a mental handicap will choose their living environment is revealing.

No doubt they will, like most of us, continue the long and complex process of search and trial, selection and change, sifting out and opting in, so that, by their mid-twenties or thirties perhaps, they will have settled themselves into a community that answers their own particular needs, among people whose lifestyle they largely share; whose outlook on life approximates to their own, whose needs and aspirations they can identify with. (West, 1985)

West argued that her 'special daughter', Lucy, should also have the right to choose her own environment. This raises the possibility that 'apartheid' policies will be allowed to continue, but such a danger should be used as an argument for vigilance, not a refusal to consider whether a particular way of living might provide the best opportunity for a fulfilled life for some people with a mental handicap. The key question to be asked is whether it is possible to give people with a mental handicap realistic choices.

The normalisation position may disregard the right of people with a mental handicap to be different. They should not have to adopt, for example, the norm of living in conventional housing. A flexible approach should not be an excuse for sinking back into 'apartheid thinking'. Whether it is a positive, chosen difference or a negative difference thrust unsolicited on to a person with a mental handicap, the same question arises: how is it possible to give people with a mental handicap realistic choices?

Realistic choice

It is often difficult to enable people with a mental handicap to make realistic choices, because they either do not have any real choice (for example, the hospital in which they have lived for the past forty years is closing down and so they have to move whether they want to or not), or they do not have the necessary knowledge on which to base their choice (for example, it is hard to decide whether one wants a flat of one's own, to live with three others in a group home, or to join a residential village setting, if one's only experience has been living on a hospital ward). These are crude examples, but they are sufficient to illustrate the point that to enable people with a mental handicap to make choices requires considerable determination by policy-makers and professionals. They must not necessarily ensure that people with a mental handicap will conform to certain roles decided by professionals, but rather that they should have the maximum possible real choice about how they live their lives.

The touchstone for the policy debate is not 'social role valorization', or normalisation, but whether it is possible to give realistic choices to people with a mental handicap, so they can live fulfilled and satisfying social lives, in the knowledge they are loved and accepted, and can love and accept other people. Any policy should be based unambiguously on unconditioned valuing of people with a mental handicap as they are.

In the process of enabling people with a mental handicap to have maximum realistic choice and to create a fulfilling lifestyle 'normalisation' will be an important tool, probably the most powerful that is available. But it must remain a tool. As an overall philosophy it is inadequate. Any attempt to treat it as an overall philosophy risks the danger of undermining its credibility. This would be a disaster, as it has been responsible for major improvements in the approach to people with a mental handicap. At the centre of any policy for people with a mental handicap should be the valuing and acceptance of them for their own sake as they are, not the valuing of a technology, however enlightened. To pursue normalisation or 'social role valorization' as ends in themselves could result in people with a mental handicap having less choice, not more.

Chapter seven

Economics and the care of people with a mental handicap

Ken Wright and Alan Haycox

The role of economics

Economics relates to the choices people make. We are all forced to make choices that are necessary because the resources (time, money or personal energy) are inadequate to provide for all the things that are purchased, consumed or completed. The role of economics is to study how people make their choices and to provide the information so that scarce resources are used in the best possible way. In this chapter the choices relate to alternative ways of providing services for people with a mental handicap; in particular, it is concerned with the information that public authorities require to allocate scarce resources to provide the best care possible to people, wherever they are living.

Choices are always necessary in public services because there are many competing claims for resources at all levels of public adminstration. The health service competes with other public services (e.g. education, police, defence, housing), for a share of the public purse. Within the health service, choices have to be made about who receives care, when, where, how, and by whom. Services for people with a mental handicap have to compete for resources with services for people who are acutely ill, chronically sick or who have social problems. Within services for people with a mental handicap, choice has to be made about the type of services available, their location, and who is to be cared for in different locations. This last set of choices relates to the way in which the resources are allocated to people with a mental handicap to provide the best possible care.

The first part of the chapter outlines the theory of economic appraisal and its applications to the care of people with a mental handicap. The second part uses a case study to illustrate the way in which alternative allocations of resources can be evaluated. The third part shows the ways in which decisions made about the allocation of resources to different services can be implemented efficiently.

Economic appraisal

The potential range of available options is large at any given time and it is impossible to appraise all simultaneously. Thus economists choose how to allocate their own resources of time and energy amongst these competing claims for their analysis. The usual approach concentrates efforts on options which use the most costly set of resources, on the assumption that their analysis will yield useful results. Nevertheless, there are still areas of economic appraisal which have proved very difficult to complete and it is wasteful to concentrate too many resources in these areas until more fundamental theoretical work has been completed.

Once the choice of options has been identified the resources used to pursue each option should be listed. 'Resources' imply real inputs of labour, land and capital (e.g. buildings, vehicles, equipment) irrespective of ownership. One distinguishing feature of economic appraisal is its insistence on identifying all resources used, since it considers the use of all society's resources, not merely those which are paid for out of the public purse. Thus the appraisal of each individual option requires the drawing up of a 'balance sheet of resources used' by different organisations and households. The effects of these uses on the welfare of people with a mental handicap also require consideration. Often an appraisal will identify the ownership of the resources, indicated in Table 1.

Table 1 Economic appraisal of alternative ways of caring for people with a mental handicap

Resource use (cost)	Effects on clients and carers (benefits)
NHS resources	Improvement in personal satisfaction
Local authority resources	Improvement in social functioning
Resources of voluntary societies	Improvement in satisfaction of carers (relief of stress and anxiety, etc.)
Other resources, e.g. individual, households	

Economic appraisals quantify the resources used and their effects on the people receiving care. This might include consideration of hours and type of labour, size and type of building, number and type of vehicles, and so forth. An evaluation is necessary of resources used and of the effects obtained with respect to their cost to society. Appraisals which achieve this aim are called 'cost-benefit analyses'; such analyses are as yet unknown in the care of people with a mental handicap. This is because many resources are difficult to cost accurately. Similarly no one has yet found a method of meaningfully valuing the impact of different types of service upon people who receive care. The usual approach at present is to complete an appraisal based on a cost-effectiveness analysis. By this approach, options are considered which either have the same cost but produce different effects of care or, more usually, produce the same effects but have different costs. The best value for money for resource usage is the option which produces the most beneficial effect in the former case and the option which costs least in the latter case.

The topics which produce the greatest difficulty for cost-effectiveness analysis are: the use of resources for which no payment is usually made (resources evaluation) and the evaluation of satisfaction with services (effectiveness evaluation). Such difficulties occur as a result of the all-embracing nature of an economist's perspective. Alternative approaches tend to side-step, rather than confront, the issues involved. For example, it has been suggested that appraisals should restrict the definition of costs to include only resources paid for by public sector agencies. This is unwise, unless the sole concern is with public expenditure. If the various options use quite different levels of public-sector resources, but the 'cheaper' options use a considerable amount of family care which is not paid for from public funds, then service development will make excessive use of this 'free' resource. There are great unresolved problems in valuing familial resources allocated to caring for chronically disabled people. It is, however, universally agreed that the cost to society of this resource is not zero, even though it may appear to be so, when considered in analyses restricted to public-sector costs (Drummond, 1980). An accumulation of evidence exists that caring over a long period can be very expensive both to the family and to the nation as a whole (Finch and Groves, 1983).

A similar mistake occurs in other forms of appraisal where the evaluation is concerned with assessment of effectiveness or benefits, without consideration of costs. The claim is made that resources should be used to provide services which produce the best effects without regard to the different costs involved. In order to make an informed appraisal, however, the analysis should be symmetrical. Benefits derived from each option have to be compared to the costs incurred by each option. Without such an analysis, an accurate appraisal of the optimum course of action cannot be made.

The objective of economic appraisal is to ensure that judgements are made on different courses of action both in terms of resource-use costs and of the effects on, or benefits to, the people receiving care. It may not be possible, given the present state of the art, to reduce all resources used or benefits gained to cash terms. However, the identification of all these factors, their quantification, and, wherever possible, their valuation, provides better information than restricted analyses which concentrate only on public-sector expenditure, or the relative effectiveness of services. It is not claimed that economic appraisal can replace judgement or make decisions for people. There are too many measurement difficulties and uncertainties in current appraisals for this to occur. The main aim is to provide better information on which to base the necessary judgement or choice.

The technicalities of measuring costs and effectiveness can be complex. The next section provides a straightforward analysis of the policy option of caring for people in hospital or in smaller units in the local setting. This analysis is then used to discuss more complicated options, which illustrate the potential and the pitfalls of economic appraisal in health and social services.

The costs of alternative forms of NHS care for people with a mental handicap

It has been accepted for the last fifteen years that one objective is to achieve a major shift from institutional care to a range of 'community-based' facilities for 'mentally handicapped people' according to individual needs (DHSS, 1971). This decision was made on the grounds that hospital environments were believed to be less conducive to the well-being and development of a person with a mental handicap than smaller, community-based environments (see chapter two). There is some evidence to substantiate this belief. Very little is known, however, about the relative costs of care. The purpose of this section is to illustrate how these costs can be calculated and compared with the cost of hospital care. Costs of care are likely to vary between groups of people with a mental handicap according to such personal characteristics as age and degree of disability. Cost comparisons have been based on various forms of NHS provision because so far there is little information on the costs of running local authority and non-statutory units. The principles of costing can be applied, irrespective of which administrative authority is responsible for providing services.

The analysis starts with an examination of the cost of hospital care and the way in which costs vary from ward to ward owing to the different personal characteristics of the people with a mental handicap who are cared for on each ward. An analysis of costs of small-scale NHS units follows, including an examination of the adjustment of the NHS unit costs. External services received by residents from various agencies are also considered. By comparing these costs, some of the major resource consequences of the move to neighbourhood settings can be examined. This methodology can thus be applied to non-NHS units, to provide a more detailed analysis of the total resource consequences of the move to local settings.

Costings are based on the current costs of running hospitals and 'community-based' units. Capital costs have been excluded, because little is known about how the hospital buildings, land, furniture, and fittings can be used following the move into new settings. All cost comparisons should therefore be considered with caution.

Cost of hospital care

NHS costs

An 800-bed hospital for the care of people with a mental handicap was selected for cost analysis. Average costs were close to the costs of other such hospitals in Britain. The hospital accommodated people with a wide range of characteristics in terms of age, sensory deprivation, and physical disability. The cost structures identified should therefore be comprehensive and nationally representative.

Details of the ward costing exercise can be found elsewhere (Wright and Haycox, 1984). During the period 1 October 1981 to 31 March 1982, 76.5 per cent of total hospital expenditure was traced directly to ward level. Where general cost allocation was necessary (for example, for administration), or where it was not possible to ascribe resources to individual people, then an appropriate average cost was allocated to the relevant ward. Cost allocations were not made to wards which were known not to use the particular services allocated. The aim of the ward costing exercise was to trace overall hospital costs to each ward. This helped minimise distortions which were introduced into the ward costings by the use of more general allocation procedures. In addition, by tracing costs over a long period, distortions introduced by exceptionally heavy short-term utilisation of services by any particular ward would be reduced.

Local education authority (LEA) costs

The LEA provided three forms of educational support to the people in hospital. The children were provided with school places and adults received either adult education or further education.

A school designated ESN Educationally Sub-Normal was attached to the hospital. During the study period the school had 49 children and teenagers between the ages of 8 and 19. All except four of these pupils lived at the hospital. Total cost to the LEA was allocated to the wards in proportion to the number of pupils taken from each ward.

The LEA provided two teachers for adult education at the hospital. To allocate expenditure, adult education teachers provided a list of the people in the hospital who received adult education. These pupils were traced to their wards and the staff costs allocated to these wards.

Further education was provided in local colleges. To estimate the cost of education received at the local colleges, the number of contact hours provided to people with a mental handicap from each ward was estimated and allocated to these wards.

Social services (SS) costs

Costs incurred for people living in the hospital by the Social Services Department were twofold. They included, first, services such as social work which were geographically located at the hospital; and second, those services which were provided within local settings but utilised by the people living in the hospital.

The only cost incurred at the hospital was that of social services staff providing a social work service. To allocate the social work costs to individual wards it was necessary to examine each 'active file' kept at the hospital Social Work Department. This enabled allocation of the total social work cost to relevant wards. The only social services costs incurred in local settings were those of one person with a mental handicap who attended the local authority adult training centre. This cost was allocated to the ward where the person lived.

Table 2 Total public-sector cost of large-scale provision for people with a mental handicap 1981–1982 (all costs in pounds)

Ward	NHS cost	LEA cost	SS cost	No. of 'in-patient' days	Total ward cost per 'in-patient' day
Children's wards					
5	148048	19331	428	3405	49.28
9	129274	16419	856	3895	37.62
17	116566	24763	–	3285	43.02
1	191230	–	–	6935	27.57
2	199593	–	–	9125	21.87
3	182858	–	–	9855	18.55
4	167784	517	–	6570	25.62
6	142241	259	1284	5475	26.26
10	190737	345	–	6205	30.79
11	250256	172	428	5355	46.85
12	281223	431	–	16910	16.65
13	117828	1937	1070	7848	15.40
14	261727	2629	3147	15878	16.85
15	341448	–	214	10220	33.43
16	270110	2692	–	9005	30.29
19	172721	259	642	9855	17.62
20	260873	1327	1499	9975	26.44
21	250417	2692	–	8760	28.89
22	233669	86	214	4818	54.13
24	286131	2765	356	14538	19.93
26	293668	22717	1713	10523	30.23
27	270457	733	–	17035	15.92
28	210952	–	856	9490	22.32
29	273120	250	428	9673	28.31
30	415466	86	1070	11680	35.67
Wards for elderly people					
7	157245	681	214	9370	16.88
8	288503	–	–	9428	30.60
18	211833	431	428	13260	16.04
23	134696	–	214	7055	19.12
25	174173	517	428	7420	23.60
Total	6624868	102039	13701	272346	24.83

Summary of costs

Total costs traced to public sector agencies (NHS, LEA, and social services) are illustrated in Table 2. No other public-sector resources were utilised by people who lived in the hospital.

Cost of NHS units in the local settings

NHS costs

This section calculates the total revenue cost consequences to the NHS for provision of residential care for people with a mental handicap in small 'community' units. Two major problems exist in isolating the costs of such units: first, the provision of different types of care, and, second, the utilisation of external NHS facilities. These problems are discussed in detail below.

Where units provided a mixture of residential and day-care it was difficult to isolate the cost consequences of provision of residential care. The procedure was necessary, however, to standardise costs and to allow valid comparisons between small units and hospitals.

It was difficult to carry out detailed observational studies to identify all external NHS facilities used by residents or non-residents. Most of the relevant information was available in the data relating to facilities and services for people with a mental handicap; the accuracy of these data was checked with unit administrators. The 'facilities data' provided information relating to the amount of time allocated by physicians, psychologists and nurses to the provision of non-residential care to the local neighbourhood settings. These staff provided the majority of services to non-residents. The identification of the actual time spent in provision of non-residential care was an important step in isolating the costs of these services.

Certain units did not make provision for the total needs of their residents and a larger local hospital was used to provide services. This external provision included special facilities such as the use of a hydro-therapy pool and specialist interventions such as physiotherapy. Where the services were provided in a nearby hospital they were both regular and intermittent. The intermittent provision of service into units by the larger local hospital is assessed in the next section.

In most of the units included in the study, people with a mental handicap had minimal involvement with NHS facilities outside their own unit. Where visits to other NHS facilities occurred this was either for social reasons or to prepare the person for an impending move into another facility. This often occurred when a person with a mental handicap was transferred from child to adult services. Staff supervision and transport would usually be provided by the relevant unit. Resource consequences for the hospital visited for these services were considered minimal. Therefore most of the costs incurred were already included in the unit's cost accounts.

Only one unit in the sample made particular use of facilities provided by the larger local hospital. This unit had ten residents who used industrial training facilities and one resident who attended occupational therapy sessions at a local hospital. Given the close proximity of the hospital, residents walked there, and no staff from the unit accompanied them. The residents returned to the unit for meals and the only known resources used at the main hospital were occupational and industrial training facilities.

Table 3 illustrates the results of this section and provides an estimate of the total cost consequences to the NHS from the operation of small community units for people with a mental handicap. NHS costs have been revalued to bring them into line with costs of local authority services based on the fiscal year 1982–83. The revaluation is 6.5 per cent and was based on the cost indices developed by the Department of Health and Social Security (DHSS).

LEA costs

The extent and type of educational provision for each unit depended mostly upon the age of the people in particular units. Provision of school places in ESN(S) facilities represented the major LEA expenditure for people with a mental handicap. However, some adults were provided with adult and/or further education services. The amount of educational facilities used by each person was traced and multiplied by the average cost per place in the relevant facility. For school provision, the average cost per pupil year in the specific ESN(S) school was traced. For adult and further education, an estimated cost per student for the particular course undertaken, including its length and nature, was determined. The work was completed with the close co-operation of the relevant LEA. The estimated costs for the LEA are given in Table 4.

Table 3 Summary of NHS costs (all costs in pounds)

Unit	Total cost (costing return)	Plus use of external facilities	Less value of service to non-residents	Total net cost 1981–82	Total cost revalued 1982–83
Children's units					
A	367554	–	–7351*	360203	383616
B	367605	–	–7361*	360254	383669
C	231958	–	–12534	219424	233686
D	324475	–	–2758	321717	342629
E	226162	–	–4520	331642	353199
F	233962	–	–14507	219455	233720
G	206435	–	–18082	188853	200596
H	168534	–	–	168534	179489
Adult units					
I	191889	–	–	191889	204361
J	191506	–	–25782	165724	176496
K	74809	–	–35978	38830	41534
L	189084	–	–	139084	148124
M	164556	–	16248	148303	157948
N	193342	–	–	193342	205909
O	162372	–	–	162772	172926
P	185714	–	–	185714	197785
Q	113753	–	–	113753	121147
R	123064	3600	–32903	93761	99855
Elderly units					
S	168852	–	–1210	162633	173294
T	147403	–	–	147403	156984
U	218460	–	–	218460	232660

Source: Unit Administrator
* Based upon estimated staff time spent on outreach facilities

Social security costs

The cost of social work support was calculated on a qualified social worker's salary at mid-point on the scale (point 27), with associated national insurance and superannuation costs at 1982 rates. This was £8,987 per annum. Assuming a 46-week working year and a 36-hour week, this produces a cost per social work hour of £5.28.

Table 4 Total public-sector cost of small-scale NHS units for the care of people with a mental handicap (all costs in pounds)

Unit	Total NHS expend-iture	(% of total)	Total LEA expend-iture	(% of total)	Total SS expend-iture	(% of total)	Total expend-iture	No. of 'in-patient' days	Total cost per 'in-patient' day
Children's units									
A	383616	(82)	80399	(17)	5931	(1)	469946	6840	68.71
B	383669	(87)	48433	(11)	8907	(2)	441089	8007	55.09
C	233686	(81)	21532	(8)	2966	(1)	258284	4526	57.04
D	342629	(88)	41584	(11)	4493	(1)	388706	5657	68.71
E	353199	(90)	26845	(7)	10719	(3)	390763	7411	52.73
F	233720	(90)	18802	(8)	4483	(2)	257015	6090	42.20
G	200596	(84)	36350	(15)	1197	(1)	238143	3979	59.85
H	179499	(90)	14310	(8)	4493	(2)	198292	2665	7.41
Adult units									
I	204361	(79)	2753	(1)	51977	(20)	259091	10197	25.41
J	176496	(88)	–	–	24270	(12)	200766	4891	41.05
K	41354	(93)	–	–	2966	(7)	44320	3541	12.52
L	148124	(88)	4733	(3)	14557	(9)	167414	4197	39.89
M	157948	(89)	185	–	19817	(11)	177950	4197	42.40
N	205909	(96)	5506	(3)	1785	(1)	213200	8740	24.39
O	172926	(91)	4523	(3)	11775	(6)	189224	9121	20.75
P	197785	(93)	–	–	15319	(7)	213104	5774	36.91
Q	121147	(86)	–	–	19466	(14)	140613	2358	59.63
R	99855	(90)	–	–	18759	(10)	110614	5879	18.82
Elderly units									
S	178204	(100)	–	–	–	–	173204	11021	15.72
T	156984	(92)	371	(1)	13588	(7)	170943	5931	28.91
U	232660	(98)	3540	(2)	137	–	236337	16180	14.61

Where the number of social work hours with particular units or people was unknown, a different costing procedure was adopted. In one authority, the average active caseload of a social worker for people with a mental handicap was fifteen. Where data relating to the actual input to each unit was unavailable, this approximation was used. Where a resident of a unit was actively supported by a social worker and the extent of that support was unknown, one-fifteenth of the total cost of employing a social worker, estimated as above, was allocated to the relevant unit. This produced a cost of £599 per annum for each resident supported.

No allocation of the cost of secretarial and direct administrative costs for social work support was included in the health service accounts. Where social work support was completed by hospital social workers, central administrative and support services relevant to social work were also excluded, owing to the difficulty of apportionment.

Many people with a mental handicap living in small NHS units made use of day facilities provided by social services departments, especially adult training centres. Many areas experienced a chronic shortage of adult training centre places and any increase in health service provision was accompanied by an associated increase in the need for places.

Where the information was available, an estimate of the actual cost of provision of specific places for residents of health service units, including transport, was used. Where the actual cost consequences of residents' utilisation was unknown, the average cost per place at the adult training centre (divided between 'normal' and 'special care' provision) was used. Average costs were used because the demand for places was not likely to increase more than marginally.

Summary of costs

The overall results of the previous sections have been summarised in Table 4. The table provides an estimate of total public-sector costs of provision of care by each unit to particular groups of people with a mental handicap.

Comparing the costs of small units and hospitals

Introduction

This section aims to analyse costs of providing services for 'comparable' groups of people in different settings. Previous work has detailed costs in providing services for people living in wards in a hospital environment (Wright and Haycox, 1984). Cost consequences for particular groups of residents in a hospital environment were also provided. These groups shared similar characteristics (e.g. age, size of living unit) which were expected to influence the resource requirements necessary for their care. Almost every characteristic of both people and living environments influences the resource consequences of care provision. The most important factors were isolated, but combined to produce a 'unit profile'. This was used to assess comparability of living units in different locations.

Classification systems and the construction of unit profiles

People with a mental handicap form a heterogeneous population. Wide variations occur in abilities, behaviour, problems, secondary handicaps and many other factors. Meaningful comparisons between living units in different locations should account for the heterogeneity of the population. The resulting problems with measurement have encouraged the construction of classification systems. However, two problems typically occur when such systems are constructed relating, first, to the factors to be included in the categorisation of residents, and, second, to how individual measures can be combined to provide an overall 'index of comparability'. Ideally, every characteristic which exerted influence upon the resource cost of care should have been included in the comparison (Wright and Haycox, 1984). Such a wide range of comparison was not practical, however; instead efforts were focused on matching wards and small units according to factors which statistical analysis had indicated were most likely to influence costs. The analysis (Wright and Haycox, 1984) identified the following main factors influencing level of costs.

1 Average age.
2 Proportion of people who were 'highly dependent'.
3 Number of beds provided.
4 Occupancy levels.

Wards and units were pre-classified into children (average age below nineteen), adults, and elderly people (average age above sixty). The profiles of units and wards were compared only within these three main categories.

Data upon which unit and ward profiles were constructed, together with each unit and ward total public sector cost per person per day, are given in Tables 5 and 6. Each unit was matched with a comparable ward according to these profiles, providing the basis for the following analysis.

Cost comparisons

Two sets of cost comparisons are detailed. Average revenue costs of the small local units are compared with the average revenue costs of the closest comparable ward. This provided an estimate of the long-term cost consequences of closing a ward for people with a mental handicap and transferring them to a small-scale unit.

Table 5 Hospital ward profile and associated costs

Ward	Beds	Age	Occ.%	PH%	BD%	D. 3%	D. 4%	Cost
Children's wards								
5	11	14	91	0	0	29	43	52.48
9	11	18	55	56	9	0	100	40.06
17	10	12	90	99	0	0	100	45.82
Adult wards								
1	18	45	100	32	21	5	77	29.50
2	25	49	100	12	28	12	67	21.43
3	27	53	100	78	33	50	36	19.89
4	18	40	100	0	0	52	37	27.42
6	14	25	100	0	80	14	43	27.85
10	20	51	85	24	18	17	83	32.79
11	15	31	100	7	61	29	57	49.94
12	49	49	100	4	22	36	2	17.87
13	15	52	80	0	0	25	0	16.40
14	46	46	93	21	23	17	2	18.00
15	28	54	100	36	11	25	37	35.71
16	25	41	100	0	36	15	62	32.40
19	30	39	90	0	41	31	12	18.82
20	28	39	96	0	0	0	0	28.13
21	27	33	89	100	0	4	92	30.91
22	11	22	91	68	8	50	50	57.78
24	45	59	89	18	23	22	0	21.22
26	28	53	100	45	17	15	4	32.15
27	50	55	90	15	9	6	0	17.08
28	28	57	93	42	15	13	75	23.80
29	28	53	93	19	15	27	23	30.15
30	34	94	0	75	13	61	61	38.02
Wards for elderly people								
7	26	64	100	39	8	9	13	18.0
8	27	74	100	62	23	35	13	32.72
18	41	68	88	14	3	6	15	17.08
23	20	62	85	21	16	18	12	20.45
25	23	61	100	5	5	4	12	25.13

Beds Average number of available staffed beds
Age Average age of residents
Occ.% Average occupancy level of unit
PH% Percentage of residents defined as being significantly physically handicapped (either severe difficulties with walking or suffering from sensory deprivation)
BD% Percentage of residents defined as being significantly (as opposed to mildly) behaviourally disturbed
D3% Percentage of residents falling into National Development Group Dependency Category 3
D4% Percentage of residents falling into National Development Group Dependency Category 4
Cost Total ward cost per 'in-patient' day

Table 6 Data for resident profiles in community units

Unit	Cost per 'patient per day'	Beds	Age	Occ.%	BD%	D3%	D4%	PH%
A	68.71	25	14	76	20	15	33	13
B	55.09	27	14	82	26	17	70	37
C	57.04	17	14	71	37	72	28	42
D	68.71	24	12	66	21	0	100	64
E	52.73	24	15	83	66	0	100	5
F	42.20	24	16	72	12	0	100	82
G	59.85	14	15	78	100	0	92	0
H	74.41	10	14	73	55	0	89	0
I	25.41	36	34	78	5	0	20	5
J	41.05	15	38	89	25	25	15	20
K	12.52	12	29	83	45	35	0	8
L	39.89	14	28	82	33	0	83	33
M	42.40	13	28	90	17	0	50	33
N	24.39	26	48	92	0	0	10	0
O	20.75	27	59	92	0	0	0	5
P	36.91	20	34	79	28	22	39	22
Q	59.63	10	27	65	0	3	0	10
R	18.82	19	35	84	0	0	0	0
Elderly units								
S	15.72	33	62	92	0	10	0	0
T	28.91	17	61	96	11	0	25	6
U	14.61	49	60	89	4	0	14	7

Beds   Average number of available staffed beds
Age   Average age of residents
Occ.%   Average occupancy level of unit
BD%   Percentage of residents defined as being significantly (as opposed to mildly) behaviourally disturbed
D3%   Percentage of residents falling into National Development Group Dependency Category 3
D4%   Percentage of residents falling into National Development Group Dependency Category 4
PH%   Percentage of residents defined as being significantly physically handicapped (either severe difficulties with walking or suffering from sensory deprivation)

These long-term cost consequences applied when whole groups of wards or entire hospitals were closed and it was possible to reduce or eliminate the 'hotel' element of costs. These hotel costs included the provision of heat, light, catering services and administration, all of which affected large groups of people and therefore had to be continued until large groups of people had left the hospital. For example, a ward required heating and lighting until the last person had been transferred. Heating and lighting in corridors and common rooms were maintained until groups of wards were closed. Given this variation in costs with reductions in the number of people, an effort was made to identify the shorter-term consequences of cost savings when only one ward was closed. These costs were termed 'marginal savings' and are detailed in Table 7. In the main they comprise costs that were traced directly to the specified ward.

Table 7 Directly traced costs as an estimate of marginal savings through ward closure

Ward	No. of 'in-patient' days	Total ward cost (£)	Directly traced	Total estimated savings (£)	Estimated savings per 'in-patient' day (£)
		£	%	£	£
1	6935	192692	80.4	154883	22.33
2	9125	201079	77.7	156274	17.13
3	9855	184356	74.1	126591	13.86
4	6570	168620	79.7	134431	20.46
5	3405	151300	77.4	117126	34.40
6	5475	145493	70.5	102553	18.73
7	9370	157306	71.4	112390	11.99
8	9428	292414	77.7	227090	24.09
9	3895	132121	69.5	9.878	23.59
10	6205	189834	82.5	156563	25.23
11	5355	249435	87.0	217117	40.54
12	16910	277606	72.6	201576	11.92
13	7848	118009	65.6	77408	9.86
14	15878	261378	65.6	171544	10.80
15	10220	343774	77.9	267689	26.19
16	9005	271620	82.2	223141	24.78
17	3285	118214	75.3	88984	27.09
18	13260	213094	70.1	149376	11.27
19	9855	171029	73.2	125240	12.71
20	9975	256693	82.7	212321	21.29
21	8760	254812	73.1	186284	21.27
22	4318	233739	88.2	206247	47.76
23	7055	131166	74.2	97290	13.79
24	14538	281706	68.1	191937	13.20
25	7420	171638	78.5	134785	18.17
26	10523	290858	83.1	241720	22.97
27	17035	270540	65.6	180292	10.58
28	9490	208947	76.0	158733	16.72
29	9673	265516	80.4	213533	22.07
30	11680	422605	76.9	325036	27.83
Total	296499	7270033	76.4	5552965	18.73

Table 8 Costs of small NHS units and 'comparable' wards of the long-stay hospital

Unit*	Cost per 'in-patient' day £	Comparable ward	Cost per 'in-patient' day† £	Difference %	Marginal cost per 'in-patient' day† £	Difference %
A	68.71	5	52.48	+30.9	36.64	87.5
B	55.09	5	52.48	+5.0	36.64	50.4
C	57.04	9	40.06	+42.4	25.12	127.1
D	68.71	17	45.82	+50.0	28.96	137.3
E	52.73	17	45.82	+15.1	28.96	82.1
F	42.20	17	45.82	−8.0	28.96	45.7
H	74.41	17	45.82	+62.4	28.96	156.9
I	25.41	24	21.22	19.7	14.05	80.9
J	41.05	29	30.15	+36.2	23.50	74.7
K	12.52	13	16.40	−23.7	10.50	19.2
L	39.89	10	32.79	+21.7	26.87	48.5
M	42.40	29	30.15	+40.6	23.50	80.4
N	24.39	13	16.40	+48.7	10.50	132.2
O	20.75	13	16.40	+20.5	10.50	97.6
P	36.91	29	30.15	+22.4	23.50	57.1
R	18.82	13	16.40	+14.8	10.50	79.2
S	15.72	18	17.08	−8.0	12.64	24.4
T	28.91	25	25.13	+15.0	19.35	49.4
U	14.61	18	17.00	−14.5	12.64	15.6

* Two units are not included because of the difficulty of matching
† Revalued from 1981–82 to 1982–83 prices

The complete results of the comparison are detailed in Table 8 and can be summarised as follows:

1   The long-term costs of children's units were on average greater than the cost of comparable wards in the long-stay hospital. There was a wide variation in cost differences (5 per cent to 62.4 per cent).

2   Costs of the children's units in the local settings were on average 98 per cent more than the 'marginal' savings expected from closure of children's wards in the long-stay hospital.

3   Long-term costs in community units for adults were 22 per cent more than costs of matched wards in the long-stay hospital. This figure, however, masks a large variation.

4   Costs of community units for adults were 75 per cent above the expected 'marginal' savings from closure of comparable wards in the long-stay hospital.

There are some reservations about these figures as follows.

1   The sample was very small: thirty long-stay wards and nineteen community-based units.
2   Choice of ward for comparison purposes was subjective. For example, there was an uncertainty in the choice of Ward 13 instead of Ward 15 as a comparison for the community units. People with similar characteristics lived in both wards, but the costs of Ward 15 were exceptionally high for its classification.
3   Capital costs were excluded from the comparisons.
4   All the units were provided by the NHS, although some hospital residents could live in local authority homes, hostels or group homes where costs were less than in NHS units.

The principles of costing care in local settings in non-NHS units were identical to those applied in the above analysis; however, the level of costs in non-NHS 'community units' was expected to be lower. A wide variety of provision was generally available, in staffed homes, hostels, unstaffed group homes or private homes. Costs of facilities such as schools, training centres, hospitals and social work services similarly have to be added to costs of non-NHS units. The range of costs was likely to be similar in non-NHS units and NHS units, except for provision such as group homes or private boarding houses, which did not have resident staff.

Capital costs have not yet been determined. The problem highlighted by this analysis is that transfer from hospital to care in local settings is likely to require increased levels of resource use, especially in the early years of change. This raises the question of whether the improved quality of care offered in local settings will be worth the increased financial cost. Estimates of the comparative quality of care provided in local settings are required to answer this question. Relevant information will become available as the numbers of people with a mental handicap cared for in local settings increases.

The economics of policy implementation

Service development and the existing system of financial control

The previous section reviewed the provision of information to assist the decision-making process relating to efficient allocation of resources. This section discussed efficient implementation of decisions. The major theme is choice and the ways in which people in organisations choose between competing objectives. Choices have to be made within certain constraints either of finance or other resources, usually labour. The previous section on cost comparisons (efficiency) discussed provision of the best care possible for people with a mental handicap and their families or carers. Staff of health and personal social services do not make this their ultimate objective. Their work and organisational rewards and penalties seem to demand the pursuit of more immediate objectives, which interfere with the ultimate objective of providing the best possible care. The result is a misallocation of resources.

A classic example is when people are receiving care in one setting, such as a hospital, but would receive better care in another setting, such as a local hostel or group home. It may be difficult to transfer them from one setting to another if the receiving organisation is required to increase its expenditure. In this example, the health authority achieves substantial savings but at the cost of increased expenditure to the local authority. Thus, an employee of the local authority who is required to reduce expenditure, and whose career prospects may well depend on achievement of that objective, may be reluctant to provide people with a mental handicap with the appropriate form of care. On such occasions, the objective of reducing an organisational budget has been given precedence over the objective of provision of the optimum form of care. Blame for this not unusual situation should not be attributed to the local authority, which is simply making decisions with reference to management dictates. The error remains in the rules of the budgeting and financing systems as they govern the course of action. The welfare of people with a mental handicap is thus at risk due to conflict of interest at several levels.

This type of behaviour distorts all decision-making, not just decisions based on cost-effectiveness analysis. Over the last ten years, the government has decided that a priority for expenditure on health and personal social services be given to people with a mental handicap. This decision is thwarted, however, if organisational constraints that operate upon individual decision-makers and organisations are not resolved. Efforts to improve care of people with a mental handicap have been restricted by problems of inter-authority resource use and the different financial rules which impinge upon decision-making processes.

This section highlights deficiencies in the ways in which services for people with a mental handicap are planned and financed. Existing and new methods of budgeting to correct these deficiencies are discussed.

Agencies should work to achieve a common objective of improving the welfare of people with a mental handicap.

Financing of services for the care of people who are very disabled is complex even for people familiar with the system; it can appear chaotic to people who are unfamiliar with the nature of service provision. A general indication of the administrative and financial responsibilities for service provision to people with a mental handicap is set out in Table 9.

Table 9 Care of people with a mental handicap: sources of funds, administration and service

Source of provision	Administering authority	Service provided
1 Department of Health and Social Security (DHSS)		
(a) Transfer payments Retirement pension Supplementary benefit Attendance allowance Invalid care allowance	Local Social Security Offices	Support at home, assistance with contributions to local authority services, private homes and hostels
(b) National Health Service (NHS)	NHS authorities	Hospitals/NHS units, community health services, family practitioner services
(c) Personal social services (PSS)	Local authorities	Personal social services
2 Department of the Environment (DOE)		
(a) Rate support grant (RSG)	Local authorities	Hostels, sheltered housing, other local authority authority housing, rent rebates, etc.
(b) Housing subsidies (HS)	Housing associations	
3 Poll tax	Local authorities	Augmentation of PSS, RSG, and HS provision
4 Personal resources Private income	—	Support at home, contribution to charges made for local authority services, private residential hospital but *not* in NHS facilities
5 Relative	—	As above
6 Voluntary sector	—	Group homes and hostels
7 Private sector	—	Board and lodgings

Although overall public expenditure plans are agreed by the Cabinet, the ways in which different agencies receive and use their budgets produce a complicated system of finance and constraints on financing. The financing of services operates at the highest level because the financing of social security and health services is controlled through the Department of Health and Social Security. Financing of housing and personal social services is determined and controlled through the Department of the Environment. In addition, local authority-based services are also funded from the Poll tax. At both local and central level, services for people with a mental handicap compete for resources with all the myriad functions of local authorities, such as education, highways, and recreational activities. In the NHS, services for people with a mental handicap compete for resources with services for people with acute illnesses and other groups who need continuing care over a long period, such as elderly people.

This system can be difficult to understand. The difficulty is compounded by different forms of financial regulation. Different forms of control exercised over real resources and expenditure produce a set of rewards and penalties which favour frugality and low service provision, stifle initiative and encourage shifting of responsibility down the line of least resistance. The best example of this is the control of local authority expenditure.

There are three sets of controls on local authority expenditure. First, there are controls on capital expenditure on buildings, with each local service responsible to the relevant government department. Thus, although capital expenditure on personal services is controlled by the DHSS, other services are controlled by the Department of the Environment, the Department of Education and Science and the Home Office. Once capital expenditure has been agreed, local authorities combine each approved 'sub-block' of money for capital expenditure into 'a single block' and then determine their own priorities on actual expenditure. Plans agreed for the building of new facilities for people with a mental handicap therefore may well be squeezed out by competition from other worthwhile claims for capital expenditure.

Second, the revenue expenditures of local authorities are controlled by a grant system which exerts penalties by reducing future grants if expenditure targets have been exceeded. Local authority dependence on grants from central government has been reduced recently. Part of this reduction, however, was due to authorities that exceeded government expenditure targets. Thus authorities who were in danger of exceeding targets were encouraged to reduce expenditure and service provision. Until recently, some lost grant revenue was compensated by increased rate revenue, but recent changes fixed a ceiling on the Poll tax to stop this practice. Thus local authority service provision has suffered severe expenditure constraints. The argument for these restrictions is that local authority expenditure cuts can be achieved by increased efficiency, rather than reduced service provision. Alternatively, it is proposed that high-priority services can be expanded at the expense of low-priority schemes, although the latter may be prestigious. The result is that growth of services for people with a mental handicap has become dependent upon the tenacity and persistence of 'local champions' who propose strong reasons to make the desired development a high priority.

Third, control of health service expenditure is similar. The grant from central to regional health authorities is based on targets which relate to previous rather than current expenditure. Some regions receive a yearly increasing grant in contrast to those regions which in the past have received a smaller share of health service resources, while others receive reduced grants. The new system of distribution may be more equitable than previously. It means, however, that services for people with a mental handicap in regions which have lost resources have to compete for a share of this reduced expenditure level with all the other health services.

Health services are subject to two controls: staffing levels and a financial control on cash expenditure. For example, if a health authority has available cash to expand services, it may not be able to do so because staffing controls prevent recruitment of the required personnel.

Two major providers of services for people with a mental handicap are therefore severely restricted in their capacity to provide more resources for appropriate services. Two other providers as yet have not been tightly controlled. Family practitioner committees, which administer general practices and the social security system, are not subject to cash limits. It has not always been straightforward for the cash-limited health and personal services to provide general practitioner care for people with a mental handicap. The social security system has allowed more imaginative responses. If services such as hostel schemes and group homes can use social security assistance to finance charges to residents, they have an improved chance of developing than services that rely entirely on local or health authority resources. Cash-limited authorities have every incentive to transfer their responsibilities to services not subject to cash limits. Inappropriate service development will occur under constraints of cash limits. For example, social security may pay board and lodging charges for people in one setting but not in another. If the total cost of the social security charges is higher than the alternatives, the existence of cash limits will encourage provision of the higher-cost service. Similarly, even if local authority hostel care is more appropriate for the person with a mental handicap and less costly than hospital care, penalties incurred by local authorities who overspend will discourage them from providing this (more efficient) form of care.

The failure to take responsibility for the efficient care of people with a mental handicap has had another highly disturbing outcome. The 'line of least resistance' along which all responsibility is passed may lead to care being transferred to families who are already struggling to provide care for a relative in their own home. The tendency to pass the burden on to families will increase if priorities in expenditure are aimed at substituting hospital care with 'community care.'

Some of these problems have already been recognised and several attempts have been made to resolve the most inefficient aspects of the present system of financing care. These attempts vary in coverage and amounts of cash released for inter-agency cost-sharing. Some of the initiatives are discussed below, ranging from the scheme with the narrowest coverage (joint finance) to that with the widest coverage (single agency responsibility).

New initiatives

Joint finances

'Joint finance' is an earmarked fund distributed by the DHSS to regional and subsequently to district health authorities. It is used where health authorities themselves or other agencies, particularly local authorities, develop services which save expenditure in the health service. Joint finance is used typically to develop services in local settings which either prevent admission to, or facilitate discharge from, hospitals. The main feature of joint finance is that it provides only short-term funding. After an agreed period, the administering agency should replace the joint finance with its own expenditure. This discourages some agencies from developing appropriate and necessary services. Despite this, joint finance has provided an essential lubricant to the development of many new initiatives. Without it, 'community care', despite its present inadequacies, would have been even less well developed (Wistow, 1983).

The principal complaint from agencies that have successfully established schemes is that the level of financing provided nationally has been totally inadequate for the demand of such funds.

The 'care in the community' initiative

The decision to accelerate discharge of people with a mental handicap from long-stay hospital accommodation to small locally-based units administered by health or local authorities or voluntary societies demonstrated clearly the problems of inter-agency financing. The government allowed health authorities flexibility in the transfer of resources from hospitals to the various agencies providing the new community-based care. Details of this arrangement have varied between regions. One interesting scheme has been developed in the South-East Thames Region. It has given district authorities a fixed annual amount equal to the average cost per person per year in the relevant hospital to provide new locally-based services. This annual sum has been distributed by the district to other agencies which provide services. District authorities have been encouraged to develop services to meet local demands, rather than to replicate pre-existing patterns:

> Thus Bromley has placed four residents in a voluntary housing scheme, Bexley four residents in a local authority hostel, Lewisham and North Southwark have been working with voluntary management schemes to manage almost all their residential accommodation except for privately rented flats, and West Lambeth have been working with joint management committees for residential services. (Korman, 1984)

The 'care in the community' initiative is an important new development in inter-agency financing and provides a much needed attempt to achieve comprehensive locally-based services for people with a mental handicap. However, there is a danger that too much emphasis is given to people who are in hospital and not enough to families who already care for people with a mental handicap, where services remain woefully inadequate. This problem is exacerbated if costs of the community care are, on average, greater than the costs of hospital care. The move to release available local cash may be drained away for other services for other people. A system of finance and budgeting is required which can use the principles of 'care in the community' to make an annual predetermined sum available for the care of people with a mental handicap. It would provide for a lifetime of care but make it available to all people with a mental handicap, irrespective of their current placement. It would be necessary to tailor the annual sum according to some 'need indicator' for services, for example, age and skills level, and to decide who should be responsible for the disbursement of the allowance, either an individual agent or a particular agency.

Agency services

Once funds have been granted on a per capita basis, as in the 'care in the community' arrangement, fundamental changes in budgeting are possible. The logic of present public budgeting and resources allocation is to make funds available to services. Funds are then distributed or rationed amongst competing beneficiaries, whether these are people with a mental handicap or other groups who require continuing care, such as people who are chronically sick. The logic of giving funds to an individual is that services then have to compete for his or her funds. Given the complicated array of services available, it might initially be difficult for someone who does not have the required professional training to allocate allowances between rival services. If such a skilled person were available, then the principle of services in competition for custom would still apply.

The attraction of this method is that the overall plan which would be constructed could include public, private, voluntary or individual services and be tailored to meet individual needs. One example of this approach is where a social worker, involved in a scheme for people who are elderly, purchases services on behalf of each elderly person subject to a budgeted maximum (Challis and Davies, 1980). The scheme is designed to help support elderly people at home to prevent, or at least delay, their admission into residential care. A similar scheme has been adapted and applied to the substitution of community care for hospital care for people with a mental handicap. This community care project aims to discharge fifty people from hospital and provide support in a range of community settings depending upon individual needs. Staff have been trained to choose and implement service packages tailored to individual needs. They aim to maximise the benefit to the client, subject to a budget constraint. The problems involved in using the 'agency model' to enable people with a mental handicap to leave hospital are more complex than the problems of supporting people who are elderly at home. People require reintegration into a new home in a local neighbourhood with new support networks. This is more complex than simply supporting and extending an existing local placement. In addition, public acceptance and willingness to support people with a mental handicap may be initially less than for people who are elderly.

Any new system should respect the independence of people with a mental handicap and their carers, who lead satisfactory lives using public services, and who take part in the work and leisure opportunities of their own choice. For those people with a mental handicap who wish to obtain more guidance and assistance in improving their quality of life, these systems produce considerable practical organisational problems. A decision is required about who will hold the budget and act as the 'key-worker'. Similarly it should be decided whether services should compete for funds and bid for customers, and how services could be tailored to meet individual needs. These problems can only be resolved after different approaches have been evaluated over a period of several years.

Single agency responsibility

The aim of single agency responsibility is to transfer responsibility for all care of people with a mental handicap to one particular agency, usually the social services department. This approach aims to overcome the potential problems arising from inconsistent or contradictory decision-making by different agencies. In addition it increases efficient decision-making; only one set of 'lines of accountability' and 'bureaucracy' have to be resolved. The House of Commons Social Services Committee (1985) has decided that local authorities should be the single agency for providing care for people with a mental handicap. This has not been accepted in the *Government Response* (DHSS, 1985) which considers that the present division of responsibilities between different agencies is correct, and that better services would follow from better inter-organisational co-ordination and co-operation. This may be accurate, but budget systems which encourage the shunting of costs between organisations hinder rather than help the collaboration required to provide high-quality services for people with a mental handicap.

Conclusion

To date, the involvement of economics in planning, developing and evaluating service provision for people with a mental handicap has been negligible. The comparative shortage relative to demand of economists with a special interest in the study of social care provides one explanation. A compounding factor is that the majority of 'evaluation' studies have concentrated almost entirely upon measuring changes in the 'quality' of care offered, without regard to costs. The scope of the economist's analytical framework is much wider.

Changes in qualitative aspects of care are an important component of any evaluative study – but only one component. Such beneficial changes need to be balanced against the resource consequences involved in their achievement. Where the resource consequences of change are ignored, there is a danger of a two-tier system of services developing between the 'haves' and 'have-nots'. The 'haves' will be those people fortunate to be in the 'evaluation spotlight'. Resources may be ploughed into improving their quality of life and, after their involvement for many years in a service that was relatively limited, perhaps such preferential treatment is long overdue. But what of the 'have-nots'? At present a fixed portion of the 'financial cake' is available for services to people with a mental handicap and, indeed, for all people using public services. An increase in the size of the slice allocated to the 'haves' inevitably reduces the amount available to the 'have-nots', wherever they are located. Evaluation studies should symmetrically balance benefits from changes with the resource consequences of achievement of those benefits. Asymmetrical studies that investigate only costs (taking the lowest cost option) or benefits (taking the most beneficial option, regardless of cost) are essentially flawed. They will produce misallocation of resources to the detriment of the whole population of people with a mental handicap.

The problems of evaluation, the development of measures of cost and the design of budgeting systems which provide incentives to maximise the welfare of people with a mental handicap as a group, are areas within the natural domain of the economist. A small but increasing number of economists have become attracted to the challenges facing the specialist in this area. There is every hope that this interest will produce better information for deciding policy, and better systems for the implement- ation of services for people with a mental handicap.

All these items were discussed before the publication of the White Paper on Community Care (Department of Health, 1989). The plans outlined in the Paper, give local authorities the lead in the development of case management systems, which are designed to provide all people with community care needs, with an individually tailored set of services to meet social care (including residential care presently financed by social security allowances) needs. Related needs on, for example, housing and health services will be met by the relevant agency in close collaboration with social services departments. Social services departments will be expected to develop new budgetary arrangements for case managers but it is anticipated that these arrangements will be flexible enough to meet local conditions.

Chapter eight

Services for whom?

Ian Macdonald

The adequacy of service provision in the private sector of society is judged by the client. If a person wants the service and has the money, business starts. If they do not want it, or have no money, business stops. For people with a mental handicap and their families, life is more complex. Statutory services do not always provide what is wanted, or what the client can afford. An attempt should be made to provide what is needed even if the client cannot afford to pay directly for that service. The service design, organisation and delivery is not simply for the provider and recipient to negotiate. This is emphasised in mental handicap, where the recipients may literally be unable directly to articulate their views. Even the expression of feelings of the person with a mental handicap may be ambiguous and open to interpretation.

The nature of the service is determined, first, by professional considerations (interventions thought to be effective), and, second, by political considerations (how much public money will be directed to that area). These two considerations are not unrelated. The history of provision of care has not been informed by direct expression or understanding of specific needs (Packwood and Macdonald, 1978). Care has generally been provided for administrative convenience, monitored by a concern for humane treatments. From the Reform Acts of 1845, through the Idiots Act and Lunacy Act to the recent Mental Health Acts (1959, 1985) the content reflects a changing attitude to care. There has been steadily increasing concern to provide humane care. Each period regards the previous regime as, at best, misguided, and at worst, cruel and exploitative.

In the past twenty years the drive has been towards 'normalisation' (Wolfensberger, 1972). For too long people with a mental handicap have been treated as disabled first and people second. Terms have moved from 'imbecile', 'idiot', and 'lunatic', to 'mentally subnormal', 'mentally handicapped', and now, 'people with a mental handicap' or 'people with learning difficulties'.

The normalisation debate articulates a value system. People with a mental handicap should be regarded as equal members of society. They should not be segregated, seen as a separate sub-species, or denied access to resources, places and relationships open to other people. This position also presumes that people with a mental handicap will be free to experience the responsibilities, frustrations, failures and rejections shared by all people.

This debate, however, relates primarily to human rights. Such debates can be found in many groups, such as women's rights and civil rights groups. It is not unusual for such debates to express mistrust in established professions and seek to challenge traditional power bases. Normalisation is also enshrined in policy documents (e.g. DHSS, 1982; King's Fund, 1980). Commitments have been made to close institutions.

A model for examining change and development

In the heat of debates and concerns about people and their future, it is easy to muddle different aspects of the problem. This confusion detracts from possible solutions. For example, it is easy to discuss the 'needs of people with a mental handicap' as if they are a homogeneous group. Three aspects of behaviour can be distinguished to facilitate change and development at an individual, organisational or societal level.

Beliefs, values and aspirations

These are usually implicit. They constitute the set of general ideas and feelings which determine the overall direction of behaviour. They are not limited by time or a particular formulation but can be changed by experience.

Bounded public statements

These are the set of formulated hypotheses which are unambiguous and testable. They are clear 'if/then' statements which have no essential, intrinsic value, other than their ability to be tested. The nature of these statements is that they are open to public scrutiny. They are not part of the internal world of private meaning but exist in the public and social world. An example of a bounded public statement would be the hypothesis that non-hospital service provision is no more expensive than hospital provision for people with a mental handicap.

Actions

These are the set of behaviours that actually occur, whether or not they are consistent with beliefs, or predicted by hypotheses.

It is only useful to separate these aspects of behaviour to examine how they relate to one another. The dynamic model is shown in Figure 1.

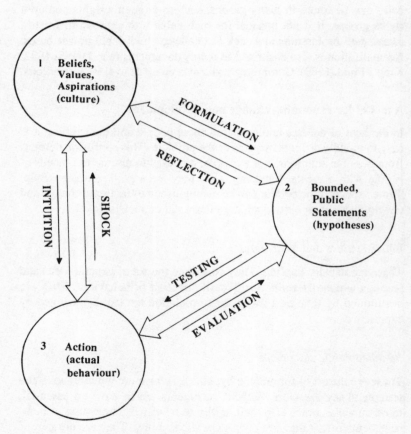

Figure 1 A model for examining change and development

In the model, beliefs and values influence the formulation of hypotheses. These formulations, however, should themselves be testable and the resulting hypotheses should not be predetermined by the values. This can make the process of formulation difficult, since it requires a temporary suspension of belief systems. The formulation process itself may result in a reflection, which in turn influences beliefs. Once clear formulations are made, they can be tested in practice and subsequently evaluated. The resultant actions may lead to an evaluation and reformulation of hypotheses, which will affect beliefs.

Beliefs may also directly affect action without a deliberate formulation of which behaviours (and in what form) will occur. Most of the time, actions occur without deliberate formulation or reflection. Actions, however, may also directly affect beliefs. For example, this may occur where a person we believed to be honest or trustworthy acts in a way to destroy that trust. This often occurs in the maintenance or undermining of stereotypes. Such influences may be profound or temporary. The 'shock' to the belief system may be modified by reformulation, that is, by trying to rationalise inconsistent actions.

The understanding of mental handicap is open to distortion by deliberately or naïvely ignoring an aspect of the process outlined.

Distorted systems

Beliefs hypotheses

(Including 1 and 2 but not 3.) This leads to the construction of models and theories which are never actually tested in action. It results in the pejorative meaning of 'theory' or 'academic' as something which is split off from practice. The response of practitioners is to point out that the 'real world' is missing.

Action hypotheses

(Including 2 and 3 but not 1.) This leads to a cold 'scientific' approach which denies the influence or relevance of values and beliefs. It is a purely rational approach, detached from personal meaning. It is essentially an amoral approach, which can dehumanise social science.

Beliefs action

(Including 1 and 3 but not 2.) This results in untestable systems which are difficult to question. People act because they implicitly believe in what they are doing. It is the mirror image of the 'detached scientific' approach. There is no logical or rational argument. Such systems are usually characterised by powerful, charismatic leaders with devout followers. The systems often wither and die when the charismatic leader leaves, since there has been no explication or formulation of how or why the system worked. Such systems are ideological, but may claim a scientific or rational status through half-formulated propositions which are so general or ambiguous that they cannot effectively be tested.

The rest of this chapter uses the basic model of beliefs, hypotheses and action to examine some current issues in service provision. It then argues for more effort to be put into making clear formulations without losing sight of beliefs or actual behaviour.

Normalisation as an ideology

Despite the poor conditions, impersonal care and at times sheer neglect (characterised by care in large institutions which have been exposed by inquiries), closure alone will not correct the situation. Successful examples of 'care in the community' can also lead to an over-simplification. It is possible that not all people will be equally suited to 'community care'. Simplification is endorsed when the argument is based on issues of inalienable rights. Rights are absolute value statements. The 'right' of free speech may conflict with the right to protect people from offensive behaviour (for example, at a National Front rally).

Rights are usually related to needs but may be implicit, as in 'free speech'. However, discussion of rights is essentially associated with the 'beliefs' domain in Figure 1. Needs are associated with the 'formulated hypotheses' in Figure 1. Confusion between them makes it difficult to sustain either position: 'Living like others within the community is a right and a need. It is not a matter about which empirical judgement can be made' (King's Fund, 1980). This not only confuses the concepts of right and need, value and hypothesis, but confounds attempts to allocate resources rationally to implement a programme of care: 'Thus the possibility that arguments could exist, that expert opinions might consider that a home in a 'normal' setting might not be appreciated by a mentally handicapped person ... cannot be contained' (Freedman, 1985).

The ideological base of the 'normalisation' debate, when it denies discussion and negotiation, results in imposition of a particular way of life on a group of people. Thus 'normal' life is idealised and its relevance to the person with a mental handicap is assumed and implicit. Normalisation can take on a sinister, oppressive quality which in the future may be regarded in the same way that large institutions are presently viewed. Criticism of normalisation implies an apology for the large, anonymous institution. Critical appraisal is seen as reactionary and as an argument against allowing people with a mental handicap a decent way of life and a chance to maximise their potential. In short, it is viewed as an attempt to restrict the lives of people with a mental handicap and oppress them. The argument is restricted to values and personal beliefs. One of the many logical slips in this ideology is to cluster groups of concepts together: 'good' versus 'bad'. 'Normal-isation' becomes an ideology when it is assumed that this approach is the only one of real consequence. Paradoxically, it can lead to even grosser simplification of categories (or non-categories), which has been one of the main criticisms to date.

The case for greater discrimination

One of the major detrimental effects of institutionalisation is that people are made anonymous (Goffman, 1961). People are treated exactly the same irrespective of need. Many approaches also risk loss of indiv-iduality. This is most directly demonstrated in the argument for 'universal rights'.

This position suggests there should be no discrimination, either: (i) between people who have and do have not a mental handicap; or (ii) within the mental handicap group. This may guarantee certain minimum standards and humane attitudes; as an ideology it can also obscure attempts to note differences, and make useful discriminations.

Western democracies are explicitly established on an egalitarian value system. With regard to citizenship, each person should have equal treatment in law, have an equal power to vote, and have equal access to welfare services. There is an equally powerful value placed on achieve-ment. This dichotomy is best summed up by the statement that 'every person should have the right to realise their potential'. It is assumed that this potential is different for individuals given varying opportunities. This belief is sharply focused in education, where the state (local authorities) ensure that between the ages of five and sixteen all people receive adequate education. This has produced other problems, relating to the 'right to choose' and different standards of education.

The current philosophies in mental handicap are not restricted to egalitarian principles. One of the corner-stones of present policy is that 'services must recognise the individuality of mentally handicapped people' (DHSS, 1982). This involves assessment, and 'discriminatory' actions on these results means people will receive different forms of care.

Services are not open-ended

There are limitations on resources; it is not possible to meet all identified needs. Similarly, there are limitations based on judgements; inappropriate services may be provided due to limited conceptual ideas.

The ideological pressure for 'sameness' can make constructive discrimination difficult. If a rational basis for action is not formulated (relative to the belief system) there are no clear agreements about what is appropriate in any particular case. Relationships and resources required cannot be specified and changed to meet different situations, since all situations are to be the same (Macdonald, 1981).

The adoption of normalisation has also included a general questioning of the relevance of certain professions, particularly the medical profession. Since need is often defined in professional opinions, the relative status of professionals becomes critical (Macdonald, 1984a). Certainly, professional opinion determines actual service delivery. The same question applies to agencies: are people working in social services better equipped to define need than those in health services? There is a competition to define 'need' and also a confusion between need as a professionally defined term, need as an absolute statement (independent of professions), and need as a 'right' or a 'want'. This issue has been debated widely by community mental handicap teams, who have consulted the client and family (Baldwin, 1986a; Macdonald, 1984b).

In recent years, particularly with attacks on the medical model, boundaries between professions have become less distinct. The body of knowledge of each profession has expanded, originally through clinical psychology and nursing; more recently through occupational therapy, physiotherapy, music therapy, remedial gymnastics, art therapy, play therapy and social work. This requires large teams, whose size influences their functioning. Evaluation of their contribution can be difficult. There is both co-operation and competition. Given limited time, it is difficult to resolve all these problems. All service providers will make decisions about the allocation of time and resources to particular clients.

At one end of the spectrum, there is an evaporation of the whole concept of mental handicap, so that all people are seen as 'normalised'. At the other end there is a detailed focus on the individual, with an attempt to identify needs. Old categories are questioned. Labelling or pigeon-holing is avoided. People with a mental handicap have previously been denied services. A service cannot be built, however, on unrelated individual needs and characteristics. The uniqueness of individuals cannot obscure commonality. The design of (and resources for) a service are based on the assumption of a 'flow' of types of need to be met. A service is not based on the random appearance of individuals, whose needs cannot be associated. Both sides of the argument present a problem; the anonymity of broad, restrictive categories should be avoided, but so should a complete reliance on individual differences. It is not possible to provide a service where no two people with mental handicap have common characteristics beyond those they share with other people. The absence of commonality precludes the development of theory and methods based on generalisations.

Categorisation

Parents and care-workers meet to discuss and share their experiences and test whether others have had similar problems: 'I feel like that'; 'Yes, she does that'; 'No, that has never been my experience'. Sharing can be a comfort; mutual recognition helps, and learning how another person coped, or failed to do so, is crucial. Prediction and meaning are at the root of these experiences: 'What can I expect?'; 'What does it mean?'; 'What is common experience?'. Learning is a result of a caring interest, which involves observation, listening and categorising. Accurate categorisation does not necessarily require a detached, administrative procedure. 'Objective' does not mean a cold separation. Rather, it can be an attempt to order what might be a confusing, frightening and chaotic experience into one which can be coped with and understood. However, categorisation without a purpose is meaningless.

Categorisation occurs all the time in daily life and enables people to make decisions. The most critical decisions relate to responsibility. Decisions about the ability of people to cope occur frequently. The education system is based on assessments of achievement. Decisions are made about the circumstances in which a child can handle more difficult academic and social tasks. Parents decide when to allow their children more scope and responsibility. At work, managers must decide how much to delegate to whom. The recipient is, however, not passive. Children, workers and friends all have their own ideas of how much they can cope with, which may or may not coincide with the views of others. In a relationship, there is constant negotiation of responsibility and power. Decisions may be agreed or imposed.

When providing services, care-workers make similar decisions, for example in allowing a person to go out alone. Similarly, the person needs to be given opportunities to choose clothes and use money.

Care as part of a service can be personalised. It is not entirely 'personal', however, in that one care-worker cannot guarantee that they will provide exclusive, continuous care to another person. If more than one service provider is involved, then there should be a rational means of communicating needs, achievements, and failures for when this information is passed on to others. Experiences are ordered and categorised in a range of constructive ways. However, categorisation can become labelling in the most pejorative sense; for example, it can be used to hide an inadequate power relationship, or an inadequate store of knowledge.

Normalisation has questioned many traditional ways of providing services. It is a critique not only of traditional systems of care but the knowledge base that underpins such systems. It has dared to suggest the emperor has no clothes and it has provided a tailor.

To investigate the design and creation of a new service requires a closer look at theories about mental handicap and their predictive power (Baldwin, 1985).

Nature of theory

Some theories are more useful than others. In day-to-day life, people have implicit theories of social behaviour to explain their world. They are based on beliefs which are based on assumptions. Probabilistic statements relate to likely outcomes of behaviour. There is more familiarity with known people and situations; the probability of a correct prediction of the outcome is higher. Often these theories are implicit. In unusual or very important situations, more care is taken to articulate expectations and consider a wide range of outcomes.

People develop by gradually accepting more responsibility in relationships. People with a mental handicap may have missed out on relationships because they are supposedly of 'arrested or incomplete development'. People who have worked in this area will report that this is nonsense. The rates of development, however, may be slower, different and at times seemingly imperceptible. There is no single theory of development used for assessment. Although Piagetian scales have been adapted there is a need to create a more sensitive stage theory as an extension of normal development. The Stratified System Theory is such a general theory. The content of such theories has not been discussed in detail; however, the advancement of theory is crucial. Unless there is a move towards a greater input into formulation then the advances made are in danger of deteriorating into polarised rhetoric in a 'backlash' of conflicting ideologies.

There are specific rituals and rules to ensure predictable behaviour at socially recognised occasions, such as conferences, banquets, ceremonies, and so on. The same process occurs in assessment meetings. These assumptions and predictions have a social context. They involve relationships and the use of discretion: 'If I do this then I feel confident he/she will do that'. A problem in the field of mental handicap is that the public and professionals are unlikely to form deep relationships with people with a mental handicap. The focus should be shifted from the person to the relationship with the person. The domain of the relationship should be specified and the 'relative authority' clarified. A relationship between a person with a mental handicap (A) and a residential social worker (B) is illustrated in Figure 2.

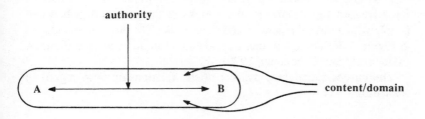

Figure 2 Relationship between a person with a mental handicap (A) and a residential social worker (B)

The content of the relationship consists of certain formulated activities: ensuring that the person is dressed, eats and learns particular social skills. The social need may be to learn to operate particular social work practices, including a method of case recording. For these relationships to exist, there will be 'legitimised power' (authority). This can be specified as decision-making. For example, who decides whether A dresses him or herself? What clothes are appropriate? Have conflicts been resolved? In summary, where is the balance of authority pivoted? Is it tilted towards A or B?

If authority is denied to A, then B defines the situation. Stereotyped assumptions can be maintained and A's behaviour will be forced into a predictable framework. This involves restricting the initiative allowed to A and restricting the opportunities to redefine the relationship. It will become a static, closed system. It seems more secure as it is predictable (especially to B).

The provision of services should be formulated, examined and questioned relative to authority relationships. Relationships should be specified and a method adopted for continuous review. The need continues to be to make judgements about who (including ourselves) can cope with what, and when we can take on (more or less) responsibility. A balanced relationship should not assume too much or too little authority. This is a central theme in 'normalisation'. Risk-taking and opportunities for personal development require careful judgement about 'readiness to learn'. The ability to make these judgements is critical when considering the appropriate role of professionals. Such judgements are on personal trust and confidence of the person with a mental handicap in professional knowledge. This knowledge should lead to predictive statements, although this rarely occurs.

A systematic model for relationships is offered in the Chart of Initiative and Independence which looks at the relationship between people with a mental handicap and their world. The chart is reproduced in Figure 3. Relationships can be understood in this way: see Figure 4 (Macdonald and Couchman, 1978).

The curves show three aspects of the relationship with regard to activities:

1   Opportunity (what a person is allowed to do);
2   Behaviour (what a person does);
3   Present potential (what a person is judged to be capable of coping with if they were not inhibited).

SCALE OF RELATIONSHIPS

KEY	No opportunity N	Complete dependency C/D	MODE A	MODE B	MODE C	MODE D	MODE E
LEVEL OF OPPORTUNITY	There is no opportunity available to do this.	It is always done for him/her.	You tell him/her when to do this and how to do it. It is always under your instructions.	You tell them when to do it but then leave them to get on, but later check how it was done.	You allow the person discretion to decide when and how to do something but you check when it is done and monitor how it is done.	You allow the person discretion to decide when and how to do something, checking when it is done but not monitoring how it is done.	You allow the person full discretion and do not check or monitor. You intervene only if requested to do so by the person.
BEHAVIOUR	I have not seen the person actually do this recently. If the person refuses to do this activity state this by noting 'R' under N.	The person does not achieve goals or plans even when told or shown.	The person only does this when told or shown what to do and how to do it.	The person only does this when told what to do but can then get on and do it.	The person does this activity without being told but when and how they do this is in a pre-set way.	The person does this activity without being told. The when is not fixed and others wishes are tolerated unless they threaten the goal of activity.	The person does this activity in a flexible way without being told they can take into account the needs of others and substitute goals.
PRESENT POTENTIAL	There is no opportunity for the person to show any potential.	The person does not have the capacity to act on goals or plans even when told or shown.	The person can only do this when told or shown what to do and how to do it.	The person can only do this when told what to do but can then get on and do it.	The person is capable of doing this without being told both when and how they do this is in a pre-set way.	They are capable of doing this activity without being told. The when is not fixed and others wishes are tolerated unless they threaten the goal of activity.	They are capable of doing the activity in a flexible way without being told. They can take into account the needs of others and substitute goals.

Figure 3 Scale of relationships

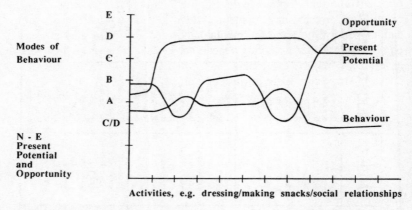

Figure 4 The relationship between modes of behaviour and specific activities

Learning opportunities frequently are limited in certain areas and it is necessary to discover inconsistencies in relationships (e.g. between what people are capable of doing, and they are allowed to do). Judgements of potential may be unnecessarily limiting and behaviour can be inhibited.

Developmental theory

The Chart of Initiative and Independence provides a descriptive model. Improved understanding of the potential and rate of development of people with a mental handicap is also required. Some people can cope with more complex relationships and feel secure with responsibilities earlier than others. Some people seem to 'regress'. It is difficult to discuss this without a shared language or scale. A scale of authority or responsibility for decisions has been suggested and explained more fully in *Stratified System Theory* (Jacques, 1989).

The meaning of 'normal' development has been oversimplified, and is often taken to mean a statistical method; it can lead to misunderstanding and mistreatment of individuals. Consideration of the whole population of people suggests certain rates of development on a scale of complexity in relationships; these are shown in Figure 5. Curves 1 to 4 represent what is statistically accepted to be within the 'normal' range of behaviour (for children in ordinary schools). However, curves 5 and 6 are also 'normal' for people developing at their own rate. Anyone can experience 'arrested development', which relates to opportunities and can happen irrespective of a 'mental handicap'. People on curves 5 and 6 (usually described as having a mental handicap) may not be 'arrested' at all. They may be expressing their potential as fully as someone on curve 1. These curves are intrinsically of equal 'value'.

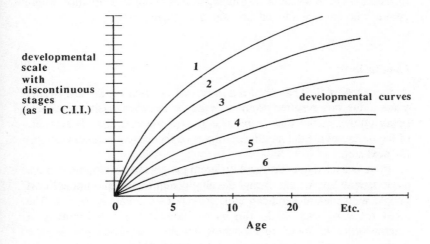

Figure 5 Rates of development

    Understanding developmental curves, (rates at which people develop) can help provide more relevant opportunities. It helps clarify what types of services are most appropriate. Even without clear, predictable rates of development, different types of relationships can be established to ensure more relevant services which are open to evaluation. All assessors, parents and friends have implicit understandings about their own and other people's potential. The articulation of these ideas into a shared scale may enable rational services to proceed.

    In the absence of a shared language of development, it is difficult to discuss for whom services should be provided. All people develop, but in different ways. Normalisation articulates the attack on the underestimation of people with a mental handicap. Many people can and will take on more responsibility in a relationship if they are allowed to develop. This is not only a question of rights. Increased opportunities to prove oneself are essential to the achievement of independence. However, 'rights' can also become a burden if people are expected to succeed in every aspect, or if expectations and interpretations of success are ambiguous. All people have areas of skill and areas of limitation. People should not be valued less because of these limitations. Further, in certain settings (outside hospitals) it is more likely that people will develop their potential. At different times people perceive the world in different ways. A sense of well-being comes about in a situation where people who have developed are valued for themselves.

Conclusions

A major reappraisal has occurred in mental handicap in the last twenty years. This has resulted from a desire to improve basic rights and opportunities, rather than from an improved theoretical understanding of the nature of mental handicap. Improved theoretical understanding is the next step.

There is a need to understand different patterns of development. Such an understanding would extend developmental theory and not split off people with mental handicap as if they were a separate species. The most relevant way to do this is to look at the development of responsibility in social relationships and how or when people take decisions according to their view of the world. This can be achieved by a clear scale of social relationships, based on responsibility and decision-making. This should encourage a shared language among carers, enabling them to communicate needs with less ambiguity. This can lead to an individual-based service (although related to a common frame of reference) which could produce better planning.

Services can be informed primarily by work that is required, rather than concentrating on physical locations, or defining services by type. Services based on identified need would lead to improved evaluation of care. This formulation is represented in Figures 6 and 7 respectively.

The development of shared language with regard to different levels of decision-making shifts the emphasis of service from a geographical to a social location. There is too much ambiguity and confusion about the terms 'hospital', 'group home' and 'community'. They imply a level of opportunity and decision-making but they are open to interpretation.

There are no precise meanings for these terms that can be applied generally; instead a new meaning must be determined for each individual case. There is too much scope for misunderstanding and delivery of inappropriate services.

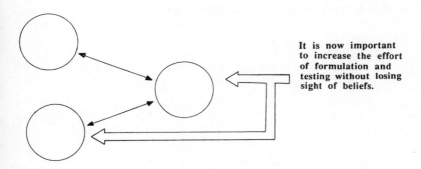

It is now important to increase the effort of formulation and testing without losing sight of beliefs.

Figure 6 Developing a shared language (1)

The structure for the formulation is as follows:

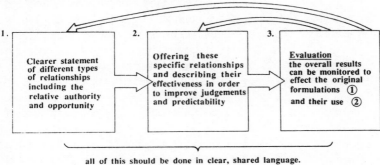

1.
Clearer statement of different types of relationships including the relative authority and opportunity

2.
Offering these specific relationships and describing their effectiveness in order to improve judgements and predictability

3.
Evaluation
the overall results can be monitored to effect the original formulations ①
and their use ②

all of this should be done in clear, shared language.

Figure 7 Developing a shared language (2)

Until such terms are clarified, actual service delivery will drift towards an ideological base and be difficult to evaluate. However, clarification is difficult as it requires people to articulate and explain their actions. Finally, it is accepted that this process is still open to abuse and any categorisation system can be used as a defence against personal relationships. It will always be important to be clear about why and when such a process is necessary, and to show that it is not merely being used as another means of control and restriction.

Chapter nine

From community to neighbourhood

Steve Baldwin

Critique of the 'community care' concept

In recent years, the terms 'community care' and 'care in the community' have fallen into disrepute amongst practitioners and researchers working in a number of areas. Staff working in services for people with a mental or physical handicap, elderly people, rehabilitation and psychiatric care have examined the concept in greater depth. This has been most visible in services that have been in transition from 'institutional care' to the provision of services at local levels. There have been, however, a number of recent examples where client groups have been 'moved out', following closure or rationalisation of institutional services, into local settings without necessary and sufficient support services being available. This alarming situation is not confined to the United Kingdom (Mills and Cummins, 1982).

The transfer to 'community care' from large institutions is flawed by a further problem. Many initiatives to transfer client groups from geographically centralised settings have failed to take account of similar clients who already populate local settings. The absence of inter-agency teamwork between centralised services, such as hospitals or hostels, and local services has increased the confusion about the means by which transition will occur. Social policy perspectives view this 'planned ambiguity' (Warren and Warren, 1977) as having a political significance; the failure to specify exact goals has allowed such initiatives to be 'hijacked'. It is significant that recent governments of different political persuasions have produced policy documents relating to 'care in the community'. In these documents the same term has been used to convey opposite meanings. Thus, 'community care' initiatives have produced quite different implications for the development of services.

On the one hand there has been a commitment to and (increased funds for) improving quality; on the other there has been a commitment to contraction, unification and decreasing costs in order to reduce quality. Failure to achieve specificity and clarity about what constitutes so-called 'community care' has allowed service planners, researchers and practitioners to share a language without a shared meaning. As a result exploitation and abuse can occur, particularly where there is a failure to agree upon means and ends for services.

'Community care' may also be understood as an ideology which is both reactionary and is essentially a 'gendered concept' (Finch, 1984). This political perspective helps to reveal the values which underpin the 'community care' concept. It clarifies the ways in which 'care in the community' relies extensively upon the unpaid labour of women during times of high unemployment. There is considerable evidence to support the belief that 'community-speak' discussions relating to 'informal caring networks', 'natural helping networks', 'good neighbouring schemes' and 'fostering schemes' have been used merely as a disguised attempt to withdraw statutory services (Finch, 1984). There is some evidence to support the belief that 'community care' in fact implies care by women (Finch and Groves, 1983; Ayer and Alaszewski, 1984). There is a danger of simply substituting the concept of 'neighbourhood' for 'community'. A need exists, however, to move away from traditional usage towards a more precise and accurate terminology.

History and development: the concept of neighbourhood

Dissatisfaction with the concepts of 'community care' and 'care in the community' has produced a new interest in the concept of 'neighbourhood'. If this shift of interest is to be useful, the neighbourhood concept should offer some solutions to long-standing problems with the previous usage of 'community'. In particular, the term 'neighbourhood' should offer clarity, specificity and shared understanding. The extent to which the concept can be refined to achieve these goals is one measure of its utility in human services.

Historically, 'neighbourhood' has been used to suggest nearness or proximity with respect to interaction with other persons. Various definitions have been proposed, including: 'Distinctive areas into which large special units may be subdivided ... such as gold coasts and slums, central and outlying districts, residential and industrial areas, middle-class and working-class areas' (Keller, 1968). This definition includes geographical relations and the concept of social class, whereas the following definition incorporates a political dimension: 'A community, market, service area, provider of shelter, arena for improving quality of life, potential force, actual or potential level of government' (Albrandt and Cunningham, 1979). Their inclusion of the word 'community' is, however, confusing, as is talk of 'neighbourhood communities' (O'Brien, 1974). In contrast, a more detailed definition is: 'A predominantly residential area of a city (i) characterised by its own economic and social institutions (ii) typified by a tradition of identity and continuity (iii) inhabited by people who perceive themselves to be residents' (McClaughry, 1980). This may be of more limited use due to its focus on city life. Similarly, 'a limited territory within a larger urban area where people inhabit dwellings and interact socially' (Hallman, 1984) is restricted to a study of urban life and does not provide a generalised definition.

Whichever definition is accepted, it should not be restricted to urban or city life, should be generalisable, and should fit with the perceptions of residents of neighbourhoods. It should also be sufficiently precise to permit researchers to use it in their work.

Users' perception of neighbourhoods

In order to avoid the imposition of inappropriate services upon clients and potential users it is important to encourage their active participation from the earliest stages. When local residents speak or write about their own neighbourhoods, there is often agreement about how environments are perceived. One way to compare the views of local residents is to request that they do a drawing of their neighbourhood, including their own house. In addition to topographical representations of physical space and buildings, residents frequently include important data relating to neighbourhood qualities such as 'atmosphere' or 'character' (Henderson and Thomas, 1980).

Important data can be obtained by listening to comments of residents. Information such as 'I didn't know where to draw the lines' is revealing, not only about the neighbourhood itself, but about different approaches to developing services. The temptation to draw firm boundaries and lines on the 'limits of neighbourhood' requires careful consideration.

The inclusion of idiosyncratic details in neighbourhood maps produced by residents reveals details about local values. Certain behaviours and characteristics are perceived as positive or negative within the neighbourhood according to prevailing values which have generally been established as traditions. This commitment to 'neighbourhood mapping' by residents confirms that planners understand 'neighbourhood' to be something personal, local and specific. There is often uncertainty about omissions, with a general agreement about inclusions.

Identifying clients

Existing provision for clients is divided into generic services, specialist services and special needs services. Generic services (for example general practitioners) tend to meet general needs assumed to be shared by all persons irrespective of age, sex, class, ethnic background, ability, status or impairment. These include needs such as education, meaningful work, relationships, a place to live and leisure. In principle, generic services should be made available to all potential users. Specialist services (for example a hostel for people with a mental handicap) often duplicate generic services by providing for many of the needs shared by all persons but providing them to particular client groups. Clients are allocated to specialist services by virtue of shared characteristics with other clients who are perceived to be 'similar'. Special needs services (such as a kidney unit) are required only by some clients with specific needs which are less common. Special needs services are not included in generic services and are rarely part of specialist services.

Users of generic services are allocated to special needs services as and when required. Membership of a specialist group such as people with a mental handicap, which results in the use of specialist services, may, however, decrease the probability of access to special needs services. Certain 'specialist' client groups may be excluded from certain services by virtue of a particular shared characteristic; for example, people who are elderly may not receive special surgery because of age and impairment.

Neighbourhood work therefore requires a commitment to develop generic, specialist and special needs services to enable all potential users to have equal access. In service systems that operate with limited funding, exclusion of some potential users may occur through a process of discrimination designed to avoid saturation of the service. A planning decision is required that will include clients in local services in a principle of 'active enablement'. This requires that clients are not passive consumers but instead adopt an assertive position in developing and using their own services.

Even the statutory services do not operate a 'services for all' philosophy. Moreover, statutory services often operate with opposing models of care. Health service models of care often assume continuity of care and offer 'life planning' for some client groups. In contrast, social service models of care are often based upon discontinuous involvements with clients, encouraging temporary, 'casework' approach to services. Joint planning initiatives unfortunately have failed to synthesise these two quite different approaches (Smith, 1984a; Smith, 1984b; Wistow, 1983).

Service provision for clients in local neighbourhoods therefore requires decisions about the inclusion or exclusion of potential users. The generalist approach (Warren and Warren, 1977) assumes that disqualification of users by discrimination is not an acceptable strategy for planning or implementing services. Equality of access exists in principle for all users across a range of services.

Identifying neighbourhoods

Knowledge about neighbourhoods will be developed through casework with individual clients and this remains the optimum method to gather information. Neighbourhood development work that is closely linked to the experiences of clients helps to avoid the disparity between the real needs of clients and the service as determined by the planners and resource holders. Casework with clients is likely to be restricted, however, by constraints of time and resources. Another means is required by which a knowledge base about individual neighbourhoods can be more rapidly established.

Warren and Warren (1977) have described methods by which an initial survey can be completed in a local neighbourhood. They recommend brief collection of data relating to housing; construction; local facilities; service institutions; clubs and organisations; churches; parks and recreation facilities; jumble sales; type and make of vehicles; window signs and flyposting; appearance and upkeep; activity level; reactions of residents; and social interaction. This approach is based upon ethnographic fieldwork and requires detailed written records of work in neighbourhoods.

Henderson and Thomas (1980) have described a similar process by which initial information can be obtained about a particular neighbourhood. They suggest initial determination of the principal features from data on history; physical environment; residents; organisations;

communications; social welfare; perceptions of neighbourhood; networks; values; economics; religious organisations; power and leadership. In contrast to the previous approach, this method draws upon participant observation techniques and requires active involvement from workers and local residents.

Whichever method is adopted, the information should be collated in a meaningful way that allows both neighbourhood workers and clients to make use of resources and services such as organisations, societies, physical facilities and key individuals. One way to do this is to invest in the production of a Neighbourhood Resources Directory.

Compiling a Neighbourhood Resources Directory

The compilation of a Neighbourhood Resources Directory is a prerequisite for much of the subsequent work within a neighbourhood. The commitment to produce a directory represents a considerable investment of resources in time and people, and the pay-offs are not immediately obvious. Some time may be saved by using existing sources of information such as census data or housing department statistics. Most data, however, are not listed in readily available forms and will need to be collected from diverse sources. Existing information may be out of date and one purpose of the directory is to provide an accurate account of services. Once completed, it is relatively easy to provide regular updates, at six-monthly intervals.

In addition to collation of existing sources of information, the Neighbourhood Resources Directory will also collect data not available elsewhere. Information relating to individual neighbourhoods permits inter-neighbourhood comparisons, with respect to the existing 'fit' between environments, resources and consumers (clients). Indeed, it is only via this process of information collection and collation that appropriate decisions can be made about the 'goodness of fit' between any particular client and his or her neighbourhood (Murrell and Norris, 1983). In particular, demographic data relating to the distribution and density of client groups, such as people with a mental handicap or people who are elderly, is required to make informed decisions about placement of a client in a particular neighbourhood. Specifically, 'resource depletion' and 'client saturation' may have reached the point in some neighbourhoods where further assimilation of clients will be impossible. This 'assimilation potential' requires careful consideration and can only be estimated on the basis of specific information relating to 'known' clients who are already users of services.

The Neighbourhood Resources Directory provides an indispensable guide for making decisions that relate to new users of local services. In particular it should provide essential information for helping any client move back into a particular neighbourhood. It is likely that information from a Neighbourhood Resources Directory will be used to make both positive and negative decisions about relocation. Some neighbourhoods are not capable of sustaining an influx of new users without additional funding, resources and development work. In this way, the directory can be used to highlight service deficiencies and gaps in existing services which should be relayed to planners, managers and administrators. Service deficiency records will help to achieve this goal.

The directory is also valuable as a teaching and training aid, particularly for new staff undertaking neighbourhood work. The need to absorb a large amount of information relating to specific neighbourhoods can be facilitated by the directory. Similarly, client and user access can be increased by making this information available in a concise format. This should include maps of individual neighbourhoods, together with information relating to the wider population, specific user groups, and a comprehensive list of known resources. Identified service deficiencies should also be listed to promote an awareness of gaps in service provision.

Identifying workers

The Neighbourhood Resources Directory provides information relating to physical aspects of neighbourhoods and is prerequisite material for assessment of 'fit' between users and their environments. Whilst this directory does contain some information relating to the groupings of neighbourhood users, however, it does not provide information about the social interaction between people. In particular, it does not give details about the social networks established or the interpersonal relationships which often form the building blocks of neighbourhood life between residents.

It is clear that some individuals achieve special significance in neighbourhoods and become 'key people' (Henderson and Thomas, 1980; Hallman, 1984). By virtue of the adoption of specific roles or duties, certain individuals exert considerable influence and power within their own neighbourhood. The formation of relationships with these key people is often a precursor to use of services by potential users or clients. Moreover, these key people can facilitate the integration of new users, providing that a trusting relationship has already been established. This involvement of key people at a local level is frequently the best way to work with forces of resistance that may be encountered when working in neighbourhoods.

Frequently, the key people whose involvement facilitates neighbourhood work are not paid workers in well-defined roles. Many of the key social interactions of neighbourhoods occur in informal meetings and in unstructured settings, such as conversations that occur in shared public places like shops and precincts. Furthermore, a considerable amount of the support that occurs in local neighbourhoods is given by friends, family and neighbours, who provide their services without financial reward (Abrams, 1980). Thus the bulk of unpaid neighbourhood work is provided by women (Finch and Groves, 1983).

In addition, some local people will be more easily identifiable by virtue of their high visibility in a defined position within the neighbourhood. Warren and Warren (1977) have listed the following as people likely to be important: the junior school headteacher; vicars; the parent/teacher association; club secretaries; tenants' association chairperson; scout and guide leaders; estate agents; local business people; the police; ethnic group leaders; and minority group leaders.

The listing of key people who hold informal and formal positions within a local neighbourhood forms the content of a second directory that is required for successful work with clients. The Neighbourhood Workers Directory is compiled from knowledge of local key people who are often 'gatekeepers' to services, or who provide substantial amounts of care themselves.

Successful neighbourhood work requires the gradual establishment of relationships with these key people. It is essential that neighbourhoods and key people are not flooded with referrals to services for new clients. Integration of new users into existing services should be gradual and should occur with small numbers of new users at one time.

It is important to maintain two separate directories. Information about workers should not appear in the Neighbourhood Resources Directory. There are several reasons for this. First, workers may wish to retain a degree of anonymity and privacy and this should be respected. Second, the pool of key people or workers may change at a more rapid rate than the information contained in the Resources Directory. Third, use of services by new users will be facilitated through established relationships between 'key people' and services. Direct contact with services from potential new users may not always be the optimum approach.

Developing neighbourhood skills

Interest in development of integrated local neighbourhood services has been comparatively recent and the 'newness' of this work makes it a soft target for criticism. Some people may fail to appreciate the differences between the concept of neighbourhood services and the established concept of 'care in the community'. Other people may have vested interests in existing concepts and be highly resistant to change.

For these reasons, neighbourhood work may not be supported by (and may receive low value from) existing systems; in some cases the work may be actively devalued. In addition, attempts to reduce or eliminate funding for neighbourhood work may occur, and established projects may be liable to 'sabotage'. In particular, staff who attempt the difficult 'role transition' involved in the development of additional skills will require support from managers and peers. In neighbourhood work the move towards development work, in addition to traditional direct-care roles, will produce role conflict (Baldwin *et al.*, 1984). Staff need to be able to cope with the ambiguity and uncertainty produced by this transition.

Neighbourhood work is also difficult because no formal theory exists upon which to test ideas and assumptions (Henderson and Thomas, 1980). Much of the written work is speculative and not based upon empirical or experimental evidence. A commitment to data collection and hypothesis-testing is therefore an essential component of neighbourhood work. This investment in comparative methods and evaluative research is a major departure from the woolly concepts of the 'community care' approach, which does not commit staff to evaluate their work. Neighbourhood work is by definition concerned with smaller units of analysis, which is helpful in evaluation research. It is necessary, however, to achieve a balance between a focus upon 'process' and 'product'. Much development work in neighbourhoods requires long-term goal planning and a commitment to record 'process data'. The temptation to focus upon highly visible 'products' should be avoided in the early stages.

An initial decision to work in specific neighbourhoods requires an appreciation of time-scales; it is often helpful to divide priorities into short-term and long-term goals. The subsequent entry into a specific neighbourhood requires consideration of many issues, including: function; goals; values; assumptions; motivations; ideologies; funding; training process; and products.

Successful neighbourhood work requires a tactical understanding of systems and an appreciation of human behaviour at many levels. Development work in individual neighbourhoods may be likened to a complex game of three-dimensional chess, where early strategies determine the outcome of later events. It is often difficult to withdraw from neighbourhood involvements once these have been initiated. Minimal initial involvement in a wider range of local settings allows for the possibility of subsequent investment in fewer specific neighbourhoods. It is difficult to avoid being 'stuck' with early success, and time-limited commitments (or project involvement with contracts) help to avoid over-investment in specific areas. Whilst it can be highly seductive to provide direct services for clients, over-commitment in this area will limit other necessary developments. Although there may be strong pressures to provide these highly visible client services, firm resistance will be required to enable other work to continue.

Neighbourhood work can occur at a number of levels and a balance is required between commitment to short-term and long-term projects. Similarly, decisions are required relating to adoption of a high-profile or low-profile approach; this will be in part determined by a focus upon 'partnership' or 'leadership' roles. It is wise to avoid the invasion of a neighbourhood by new workers; infiltration into local settings by paid staff who do not live in the neighbourhood should be achieved gradually. Resolution of some of these issues will be determined by the 'employer mandate'; care will be required in order to fulfil a fixed contract with the employer and to provide direct services for clients. Additional development work may be required in order to provide the 'setting conditions' for other work to follow. This development work is often not highly visible and does not produce obvious benefits to the users or the system in the short term. It is, nevertheless, vital to successful neighbourhood service provision in the long term.

A commitment to data collection and routine evaluation is essential to answer questions relating to effectiveness and utility of neighbourhood work. It also helps avoid the tendency of systems to exist in 'planned ambiguity'. Units of analysis considered in evaluation research (e.g. satisfaction ratings by clients; economic costs to neighbourhood; service deficiencies; satisfaction ratings by workers) should include data about individual users, as well as at the level of the neighbourhood. It is the multiple focus upon individuals, groups of users and the neighbourhood itself that provides a major strength of this approach to human services. Existing forms of evaluation tend to focus on single sources to obtain data about services. Data collection and routine evaluation can also provide the basis for rational service planning, together with relevant measures for ensuring responsibility and accountability within the system. Data collection should provide a baseline for future monitoring and evaluation; it should not become a retreat from action or a substitute for actual work.

Skilled work in neighbourhoods requires flexibility in a range of areas. The neighbourhood worker must be interpreter; communicator; enabler; guide; facilitator; encourager; catalyst; broker; mediator; stimulator; organiser; negotiator; bargainer; advocate; expert; and activist (Henderson and Thomas, 1980). Decisions relating to choice of goals and rate of progress require careful consideration; it is likely that both immediate and delayed goals to achieve change will be adopted in parallel. Various reactions to this work should be anticipated, including initial fear, hostility or suspicion. Active involvement of 'key people' at an early stage will overcome some resistance. Early 'probes' into the climate of the neighbourhood will help to anticipate these natural and predictable reactions. The skilled worker will be sensitive to feedback from local residents and users, modifying his or her approach accordingly.

The formation of new networks and the maintenance of existing relationships will demand considerable investments of personal time and energy; short cuts should be used sparingly and with caution. This need for long-term investment requires rational decisions about the focus for short-term efforts, and in most cases existing users or potential clients are well-placed to provide much of the information that should determine the behaviour of planners and neighbourhood workers. This approach, when combined with methods to improve communication, can move towards the development of user-led services in preference to the more usual services (Praill and Baldwin, 1986).

In order to legitimise these procedures, and to guarantee the active participation of existing users, it is essential to negotiate an agreed constitution for each neighbourhood. This will require regular consultation with both existing and potential clients. Natural leaders within local neighbourhoods should be encouraged to accept responsibility for this process of partnership. The constitution should be limited initially to general statements, but should gradually evolve to achieve a degree of specificity that includes both short- and long-term goals. Choice of goals is likely to reflect the value systems of the people involved in the processes of consultation and partnership. The views of users, workers, planners, and managers should be included, in order to achieve a balance and a full representation of interest groups whose preferences may be in conflict. Any conflict should be addressed through the process of consultation.

Development work towards the establishment of neighbourhood services requires considerable energy and resource investment. Still greater efforts are required to maintain such services. Workers must respond flexibly to varying demands for support, facilitation and 'active enablement' of users/clients. Neighbourhood involvement is a profoundly political activity and workers should consider their own position both with respect to their employers and their client group. Conflicts of interest are inevitable in this situation and workers should be encouraged to recognise their own needs when working in neighbourhoods. Scapegoating should be avoided as this process does not produce positive consequences either for the individuals concerned or for the system. In order to ensure that personal or professional advancement is not achieved at the expense of either the users or the system, neighbourhood workers should acquire the skills to make their own values explicit to others.

Teaching and training

Whilst 'specialists' involved in neighbourhood work will bring their own repertoire of skills to the local setting, general skills common to all workers should also be acquired. 'Resource skills' that relate to acquisition, improvement, conservation, administration or provision of services are essential to successful neighbourhood work. Common teaching or training will be required to allow a range of workers with different backgrounds to acquire common skills. Workers should also become much more discriminating to enable them to make a rational appraisal of relative advantages and disadvantages of options. This includes an appreciation of cost-benefit analysis techniques to enable workers to estimate likely advantages and disadvantages of particular options. Skills in the timing of interventions in neighbourhoods will ensure optimum use of a shifting climate in local settings (Repucci, 1977; Repucci and Saunders, 1979). Techniques such as the calculation of probabilities, decision trees and critical path analysis techniques should be used.

Some neighbourhood work will be discontinuous and evaluation will help planners to make rational decisions about when contact with a particular neighbourhood should be terminated. An initial agreement that specifies time limits, a contract and specific 'project' involvement will assist this process. Neighbourhoods may show various responses to discontinued contact, including those associated with loss, grief or separation; they may even 'go critical' to prevent the departure of workers (Warren and Warren, 1977). Where contact must be stopped it should be planned, negotiated and implemented as a rational response to feedback and relevant data. Neighbourhood workers will require specific teaching packages to become skilled in these areas.

Interdisciplinary teamwork

One major unresolved problem of the so-called 'community care' approach is that provision for users has frequently been made available only through specialist services. This specialisation of provision has produced structures such as 'community elderly teams' (CETs) in services for people who are elderly; 'community mental handicap teams' (CMHTs) for people with a mental handicap; and 'community alcohol teams' (CATs) for people with drink problems. A range of teams may co-exist in close geographical proximity and may even share facilities for meetings. The functions of such teams are diverse and may include service development work, as well as casework and referral decisions. Membership of such teams varies widely according to locality; most 'community teams', however, rely heavily upon full-time staff in 'traditional' posts, such as social workers, psychiatrists, psychologists and community nurses, to provide substantial inputs.

Establishment of community teams has helped to shift the focus of both services and staff away from institutional settings and although many team members are still based in traditional settings, most teams meet away from hospital environments. Indeed, many of the staff who make up community teams have been health service professionals, with relatively recent inclusion of social services staff. This health bias has frequently been mirrored in both the form and content of community teams, sometimes to the exclusion of other interests such as voluntary services, education services or consumer groups.

Whilst they represent different specialist user groups, these multi-disciplinary teams share some common features. Multidisciplinary teams consist of a range of professional specialists who aim to represent the client within their own field. Team members tend to produce separate programme plans for clients or users and, unfortunately, clients tend not to be present or personally represented within multidisciplinary teams (Parham *et al.*, 1977). Successful neighbourhood work demands a delicate balance between formal services and existing informal services (Abrams, 1978; Abrams, 1980). Neighbourhoods have been defined in terms of 50 to 5,000 users, depending upon local conditions and perceptions (Hallman, 1984), whereas teams for communities have been based on populations from 90,000 up to 250,000 potential users. In summary, community teams tend to: maintain specialist service provision; offer services to very large numbers of potential clients; promote multidisciplinary team-work; provide services to very large geographical areas of up to several hundred square miles.

Attempts to establish neighbourhood teams to tackle a combination of service delivery and development issues have required intensive efforts, particularly with regard to maintenance (Baldwin *et al.*, 1984). Greater flexibility is required over issues such as membership and control. Traditional expectations and practices have been restrictive in these more local settings. In particular, more involvement of nonstatutory workers and consumers has required previous methods of teamwork to be abandoned in favour of shared decision-making and a wider perspective on service provision. Some neighbourhood workers have adopted an 'interdisciplinary teamwork' approach (Parham *et al.*, 1977) which contrasts with traditional methods.

An interdisciplinary team assigns equal value to all disciplines and team members, irrespective of perceived status. Specialists do not head these teams as of right and many teams rotate the chairperson. The interdisciplinary approach also promotes the active involvement of carers, including staff, friends of clients and family members, to ensure that their views are represented in decision-making. In contrast to other approaches, one overall programme plan is agreed with the active participation of the user or their advocate. Team members implement components of the programme according to the decisions made at the team meetings. Membership of a neighbourhood team is determined by client needs and not by a particular position as a paid worker. In summary, neighbourhood teams tend to: adopt a generic approach, involving specialists but not confined to specialist service provision; offer services to a small number of potential users; promote 'interdisciplinary' teamwork; provide services to small geographical areas, often less than one square mile.

Advocacy

People who work in human services frequently experience a conflict of interests between their own needs and those of their clients. It is essential to recognise that paid workers derive an income as well as personal or professional benefits from their interactions with clients. In a literal sense, the dependence of service users provides employment for a range of paid staff (Armstrong, 1982). One response to this potential conflict is to establish a system whereby an independent lay advocate is appointed. Such a system is essential when services are developed for client groups who are unable to represent their own interests, such as people who are confused, or people with a mental handicap. Such 'citizen advocacy' systems can help to avoid the situation where services are developed and implemented for users and clients without their active involvement or consultation. A variation on citizen advocacy is the process of self-advocacy which enables clients to assert their own rights and needs without a second person appointed for this purpose. Both citizen advocacy and self-advocacy aim to promote and maximise the independent representation of clients.

Allies and adversaries

Many workers in human services maintain links or membership with other formal organisations, such as trade unions, recreation societies, clubs, and so forth. In most cases staff will be able to separate their primary work responsibilities from other allegiances. At times, however, a conflicts of interest is produced through membership of other organisations, for example when a trade union member is instructed to take industrial action, although this will produce negative consequences for clients. Staff who represent the views of organisations that are not aligned with statutory services, such as private-sector services, may experience conflicts of interest in work settings. In particular, they may find it difficult truly to represent the best interest of clients, given their own vested interests. Clearly, it is not possible for workers to exclude all other interests, although paid workers have a responsibility to represent the clients' views and interests. The responsibilities of informal or nonstatutory workers are less clear.

Similarly a conflict of interest can occur whenever a worker is bound by an employer mandate to achieve specific goals which are inconsistent with representation of an individual client's needs. Neighbourhood workers are likely to experience conflicts with regard to representation of the various needs of clients, other users who are not clients, the employer mandate and wider neighbourhood goals. Where uncertainty exists regarding priority between different interest groups, the interests of the immediate client group should generally take precedence.

Successful neighbourhood work must avoid the pitfalls of so-called 'care in the community' initiatives, where direct-care staff and managers within the same system have adopted opposing and mutually exclusive methods to implement a common strategy (Baldwin, 1986a; Praill and Baldwin, 1986). The success of neighbourhood work is directly dependent upon an explicit commitment to specific goals within an agreed constitution. The essence of neighbourhood work is the high degree of specificity that can be achieved through planning and implementing services for a small group of users at the local level.

Neighbourhood developments should be determined by the likely benefits both to potential clients and to existing users. At times, these interests can conflict. It is often difficult to detect the true mission of human services; policies of integration or deinstitutionalisation may conceal a hidden motive to reduce funding or resources (Baldwin, 1985). Methods are required to investigate and evaluate the predominant 'value transmission' that occurs in human services. Formal systems that are based upon the values of 'care' and 'helping' do not always promote these values in services provided to clients. The experiences of paid staff in such organisations are often very revealing about the values of the wider system. Many staff tolerate highly devaluing and dehumanising conditions that can be traced back to the organisational value system.

There is rarely a single value system in neighbourhoods, although there is some evidence that some neighbourhoods share common attributes (Warren and Warren, 1977). Evidently not all the neighbourhoods are characterised by the informal caring networks which help achieve integration in cohesive neighbourhoods (Froland et al., 1981). Indeed, some neighbourhoods are perceived as extremely hostile by both residents and workers. Careful consideration is therefore required when planning for clients to enter services in new settings; a process of matching is necessary to mesh clients' needs with predominant neighbourhood values.

Developing consumer-orientated services

As already noted, neighbourhood work is a highly political activity. The associated shift to interdisciplinary teamwork requires new skills to be acquired which are not part of the repertoire of most paid staff. Existing services have not always been developed as components of an overall plan but have been part of the evolution of local responses to problems or crises. Many traditional services are determined by senior planners who aim to provide for groups of people and do not use data from service evaluations to influence their views. This can lead to the crushing of innovation and the promotion of purely cosmetic changes.

A move to consumer-orientated, local, comprehensive provision requires services to be planned for individuals, not for groups of clients. These services must have a degree of flexibility and responsiveness often absent from traditional services. The active participation of consumers requires a non-hierarchical (bottom-up) approach, with a commitment to monitoring and open access to the information and data collected. Innovation and planned diversity require active rewards. Staff and carers need to cope with high levels of uncertainty, ambiguity and conflict during this period of transition. Staff training within the framework of a clear philosophy, and an agreed process of assessing individual client needs, should be available to all neighbourhood staff on a rolling programme (Harding *et al.*, 1986). The service system should ideally reward staff for effort and positive attempts to change.

Time perspectives and priorities

Establishment of local, comprehensive neighbourhood services should be based upon a principle of open access by consumers and potential clients. Only saturation of the services would justify temporary exclusion of any client. In practice, such saturation should provide a stimulus for the development of additional services to meet new consumer demands. There are, however, two main exceptions to this pattern. First, people may only be temporary or discontinuous users of services, which imposes limits on planning. Second, finite limits are often set upon resources and finance, which restrict growth and service development.

The concept of discontinuous usage is essential for rational planning and development of neighbourhood services. Where consumers enter or leave the neighbourhood, this can create a variation in demand for particular services such as education or housing. These changing demands for generic services usually reflect the actual numbers of people who occupy neighbourhoods. In addition there may also be discontinuous demands for services by virtue of the nature of the clients' impairments. Temporary or transient usage by consumers who are impaired or disabled may help to avoid secondary 'handicapping' that results from labelling a person. Even with a 'fixed' impairment such as blindness, a client's requirements for special needs services does not remain static, as further skill acquisition or improved facilities may decrease demand for services.

The second major constraint upon the development of neighbourhood services is the concept of finite resources. This concept implies a fixed amount of finance and materials with which to provide services for consumers. This is common in statutory services, such as health and social services, where a fixed budget is allocated. More recently the implementation of budget cuts has required managers to 'rationalise' (*sic*) services, often involving a reduction. The availability of finite resources has helped to produce a renewed appreciation of services and a focus upon cost-effectiveness and efficiency. It is important, however, to avoid allowing finite resource allocations to stifle all initiatives. Resources can be diverted from elsewhere, for example the re-allocation of a defence budget to health service funds. Political activity by consumers may also assist increased funding for particular services. In considering human resources there is no clear, fixed limit upon the amount of time that can be invested within the neighbourhood. Indeed, there is some evidence that more people have become 'providers' of services to other people, as well as 'consumers' in their own right within neighbourhoods (Hallman, 1984).

Data and evaluations

Successful neighbourhood work requires a commitment to the collection of meaningful data and an investment in evaluation. It is this feature of comparison (and subsequent evaluation) that distinguishes neighbourhood work from other approaches to service design. The complexity of neighbourhood work requires data collection which represents the views of users, workers, the system, and, where possible, potential clients. This helps to develop a systematic view of the total service. Data should represent both quantitative and qualitative information about neighbourhood services. The use of time-limited interventions and contracts is recommended to avoid over-investment in specific areas.

Two step-by-step models of evaluation are offered to assist attempts at evaluation. The first model offers a straightforward account of evaluation which is based upon a hypothesis-testing approach to problem-solving. The second model offers a more sophisticated understanding of the evaluation process, including consideration of the wider context in which the neighbourhood work occurs.

Problems with the evaluation of neighbourhood services

The commitment to neighbourhood work has been a recent initiative in the United Kingdom, although some examples of established services have been reported. Much of this work is based upon the provision of specialist services which contrasts with the generic/special needs approach of true neighbourhood services. Despite this limitation, however, some local initiatives have produced promising results. Other neighbourhood schemes appear to have floundered in the initial stages due to problems of service design, management and implementation.

One attempt to describe a set of local, comprehensive services provides an example of the way in which new initiatives can be meshed with previously established services (Bayley *et al.*, 1985). This series of reports provides a descriptive study of one local attempt to work with existing service systems to enable change to occur. The study does not provide data for evaluation research. It does, however, describe many of the principles of service design which may be seen as prerequisites of high-quality services. The study describes in detail one attempt to synchronise statutory and voluntary services, with a focus upon comprehensive generic services for a range of consumers.

Baldwin and colleagues reported on attempts to develop services for people with a mental handicap in local neighbourhoods (Baldwin *et al.*, 1984). This descriptive study does not produce data for evaluation research, but instead offers a process account of development of comprehensive, locally-based services for a particular group of consumers. The study describes some of the difficulties involved in a transition from use of specialist to generic/special needs services. The report outlines some of the problems encountered with the establishment of neighbourhood teams within an existing structure of 'community services'.

A research study which evaluated the transition to neighbourhood services for elderly people provides an example of system breakdown (Baldwin *et al.*, 1985; Baldwin, 1986a). The study documented the experiences and quality of life of elderly people who were transferred to a new neighbourhood 'assessment unit'. Collection of detailed data on a range of services, including occupational therapy, day-care, transport, health screening and home help service, demonstrated that the elderly people received less services, and that their quality of life (as measured by their personal satisfaction, range of services and ability to exert control) was diminished, as a result of admission to the neighbourhood unit. The research study highlights problems with the establishment of specialist services and demonstrates the need for continuing data collection to enable rational planning of services.

A descriptive study by Cadman and colleagues provides an account of an attempt to establish a local neighbourhood mental health service (Cadman, 1986). The project was established with a firm commitment to data collection to assist service planning and implementation. Descriptive accounts of the new service discussed problems encountered in the transition to new structures, providing both process and outcome data. Neighbourhood work was described from the perspective of an interdisciplinary team set up to establish and evaluate comprehensive locally-based services for a range of consumers.

Other initiatives from specific professional groups have produced a welcome move towards the establishment of neighbourhood services for a range of consumer groups. Within nursing, for example, a recent consultation document has proposed the establishment of 'neighbourhood nursing services' (Cumberledge, 1986). Whilst there are some differences between this predominantly NHS model and other generic neighbourhood approaches (such as the investment in specialist services and the dominance of a medical model), the document is a promising initiative with important implications for existing nursing services.

Multi-level needs assessment

A commitment to evaluation of service quantity requires an effective monitoring system which records relevant data as a systematic process. Many such problem-based assessments and skills instruments exist and there is a range of sophisticated options. Most such instruments, however, are limited by a narrow focus upon the client as both the source and the solution to the problem or deficit. Many instruments provide excellent accounts of the person and possible goals or objectives for change, but are restricted by failing to specify complementary targets required to sustain behaviour change. In particular, it is essential to plan actively for associated change in the people who work with the client and to create environmental changes within the wider system to maintain this behaviour.

One such approach has been the recent development of multi-level needs assessments, which attempt to specify behaviour change goals at a range of levels (Harding *et al.*, 1986). The instrument aims to avoid the pitfalls which accompany a restricted focus upon client change. Instead, it specifies the necessary change to assist the maintenance and generalisation into new settings and across time. It also helps to generate meaningful data which is specific to the needs of the individual consumer. This approach will produce relevant data both from workers who support the client, and from the neighbourhood in which they exist.

Quality of life measurement

Neighbourhood work requires a commitment to a focus upon quality as well as quantity variables for consumers. In addition to the measurement of level, diversity and quality of service components, it is essential also to monitor the 'quality of life' for consumers.

Quality of life measurement assumes active involvement of consumers in the process of evaluation. The approach is based upon a description of the 'goodness of fit' between consumers and their environments (Murrell and Norris, 1983). It enables a consideration of both quantity and quality of interactions between people in various neighbourhood settings. The quality of life measurement assumes that failure of individuals to mesh with their physical settings necessitates change within the environments, rather than focusing just upon the person.

Consideration of quality of life measurement is consistent with other contemporary attempts to measure holistic and ecological variables. It also helps to focus evaluation work upon more general factors which influence the life of individual consumers. It is complementary to the approach which uses multi-level needs assessments and goal-planning to focus upon the details of consumers' lives. Quality of life measurement aims to answer more general questions about relative standards; it is still, however, in its infancy.

References

Abrams, P. (1978) *Neighbourhood Care Social Policy: A Research Perspective.* Beckhampstead, The Volunteer Centre.
——(1980) 'Social Change, Social Networks and Neighbourhood Care', *Social Work Services*, 22 February, 12-23.
Albrandt, R.C. and Cunningham, J.V. (1979) *A New Public Policy for Neighbourhood Preservation.* Praeger, New York.
Allen, Marjory (1945) *Whose Children?* Simpkin & Marshall, London.
Anderson, D. (1982) *Social Work and Mental Handicap.* Macmillan, London.
Armstrong, D. (1982) *Political Anatomy of the Body: Medical Knowledge in Britain in the Twentieth Century.* Cambridge University Press, Cambridge.
Atkinson, D. (1982) 'Distress Signals', *Community Care*, 421-423.
Ayer, S. and Alaszewski, A. (1984) *Community Care and the Mentally Handicapped: Services for Mothers and their Mentally Handicapped Children.* Croom Helm, London.
Baldwin, S. (1985) 'Models of Service Delivery: An Assessment of Some Applications and Implications for People who are Mentally Retarded', *Mental Retardation*, 23, 6-12.
——(1986a) 'Problems with Needs – Where Theory meets Practice', *Disability, Handicap and Society*, 1(2), 139-145.
——(1986b) 'Systems in Transition: The First 1000 Elderly Clients', *International Journal of Rehabilitation Research*, 9, 43–52.
Baldwin, S., Baser, C., and Pinka, A. (1985) 'The Emperor's New Clothes', *Nursing Times*, and *Community Outlook*, February, 19-21.
Baldwin, S., Robins, J., Harker, B., and Robb, P. (1984) 'The Place Invaders: Establishing Neighbourhood Teams for People with Mental Handicap in Sheffield', *Journal of Community Education*, 3(2), 19-25.
Bank-Mikkelsen, N.E. (1969) 'A Metropolitan Area in Denmark: Copenhagen', in R. Keugel and W. Wolfensberger (eds) *Changing Patterns in Residential Services for the Mentally Retarded.* President's Committee on Mental Retardation, Washington, DC.
Barton, R. (1959) *Institutional Neurosis*, John Wright, Bristol.
Baumeister, A.A. (1981) 'Mental Retardation Policy and Research: The Unfulfilled Promise', *American Journal of Mental Deficiency*, 85, 449-456.

References

Bayley, M. (1973) *Mental Handicap and Community Care: A Study of Mentally Handicapped People in Sheffield*. Routledge & Kegan Paul, London.

Bayley, M., Seyd, R., and Tennant, A. (1985) *Dinnington: The Final Report*. Department of Sociology, Sheffield University, Sheffield.

Becker, H. (1973) *Outsiders: Studies in the Sociology of Deviance* (revised edition). The Free Press, New York.

Bellamy, G.T., Horner, R.H., and Inman, D.P. (1979) *Vocational Habilitation of Severely Retarded Adults*. University Park Press, Baltimore.

Bercovici, S.M. (1983) *Barriers to Normalization*. University Park Press, Baltimore.

Berkson, G. and Landesman-Dwyer, S. (1977) 'Behavioral Research on Severe and Profound Mental Retardation (1955-1974)', *American Journal of Mental Deficiency*, 81, 428-454.

Birenbaum, A. (1975) 'The Changing Lives of Mentally Retarded Adults', in M.J. Begab and S.A. Richardson (eds) *The Mentally Retarded and Society: A Social Science Perspective*. University Park Press, London.

Blunden, R. (1984) 'Behavior Analysis and the Design and Evaluation of Services for Mentally Handicapped People', in S. Breuning, J. Matson, and R. Barrett (eds) *Advances in Mental Retardation and Developmental Disabilities, vol. 2*. JAI Press, Greenwich, Connecticut.

Boles, S.M. and Bible, G.H. (1978) 'The Student Service Index: A Method for Managing Service Delivery in Residential Settings', in M.S. Berkler, G.H. Bible, S.M. Boles, D.E.D. Deitz, and A.C. Repp (eds) *Current Trends for the Developmentally Disabled*. University Park Press, Baltimore.

Bowling, A. (1981) *Delegation in General Practice*. Tavistock, London.

Brethower, D.M. (1980) *Behavioral Analysis in Business and Industry: A Total Performance System*. Behaviordelia, Kalamazoo, Michigan.

Bucher, R. and Stelling, J. (1977) *Becoming Professional*. Sage, London.

Buckley, S. (1985) 'The Effect of Portage on the Development of Down's Children and their Families: An Interim Report', in B. Daly, J. Addington, S. Kerfoot, and S. Sigston (eds) *Portage: The Importance of Parents*. Nelson, Windsor.

Cadman, T. (1986) 'Powell Street Neighbourhood Centre', unpublished paper, NMHA, Manchester.

Cameron, R.J. (1985) 'A Problem-Centred Approach to Family Relations', in B. Daly, J. Addington, S. Kerfoot, and S. Sigston (eds) *Portage: The Importance of Parents*. Nelson, Windsor.

Campaign for the Mentally Handicapped (1973a) *Listen*. CMH, London.

Campaign for the Mentally Handicapped (1973b) *Participation*. CMH, London.

Cassee, E. (1975) 'Therapeutic Behaviour, Hospital Culture and Communication', in C. Cox and A. Meade (eds) *A Sociology of Medical Practice*. Collier-Macmillan, London.

Challis, D. and Davies, B. (1980) 'A New Approach to Community Care for the Elderly', *British Journal of Social Work*, 10, 1-18.

Checkland, P.B. (1972) 'Towards A System-based Methodology for Real-world Problem-solving', *Journal of Systems Engineering*, 3, 87-116.

——(1981) *Systems Thinking, Systems Practice*. John Wiley & Sons, Chichester.

Cherniss, C. (1980) *Staff Burnout: Job Stress in the Human Services*. Sage, Beverley Hills.

Clarke, A.D.B. and Clarke, A.M. (1974) *Mental Deficiency: The Changing Outlook* (3rd edn). Methuen, London.

Collins, M. and Collins, D. (1974) *Kith and Kids*. Souvenir Press, London.

Cumberledge, J. (1986) *Neighbourhood Nursing – A Focus for Care*. HMSO, London.

Cunningham, C.C. (1979) 'Parent Counselling', in M. Tredgold (ed.) *Mental Retardation*. Balliere Tindall, London.

——(1983) 'Early Support and Intervention: The HARC Infant Programme', in P. Mittler and H. McConachie (eds) *Parents, Professionals and Mentally Handicapped People*. Croom Helm, London.

Cunningham, C.C. and Jeffree, D.J. (1977) *Working with Parents: Developing a Workshop Course for Parents and Young Mentally Handicapped Children*. National Society for Mentally Handicapped Children (North-West Region), Manchester.

Cunningham, C.C., Morgan, P.A., and McGuken, R.B. (1984) 'Down's Syndrome: Is Dissatisfaction with Disclosure of Diagnosis Inevitable?', *Developmental Medicine and Child Neurology*, 26, 33-39.

Dally, G. (1983) 'Ideologies of Care: A Feminist Contribution to the Debate', *Critical Social Policy*, 3, 2.

Daly, B., Addington, J., Kerfoot, S., and Sigston, A. (eds) (1985) *Portage: The Importance of Parents*. Nelson, Windsor.

Department of Education and Science (1975) *Special Educational Needs*. HMSO, London.

Department of Health and Social Security (1971) *Better Services for the Mentally Handicapped*. HMSO, London.

——(1981) *Report of a Study on Community Care*. HMSO, London.

——(1982) *Care in the Community: A Consultative Document for Moving Resources for Care in England*. HMSO, London.

——(1985) *Government Response to the Second Report from Social Services Committee, 1984-1985 Session: Community Care with Special Reference to Adult Mentally Ill and Mentally Handicapped People*. HMSO, London.

Dexter, L.A. (1964) 'On the Politics and Sociology of Stupidity in our Society', in H.S. Becker (ed.) *The Other Side: Perspectives on Deviance*. The Free Press, New York.

Drummond, M.F. (1980) *Principles of Economic Appraisal in Health Care*. Oxford University Press, Oxford.

Edelwich, J. and Brodsky, A. (1980) *Burnout: Stages of Disillusionment in the Helping Professions*. Human Sciences Press, New York.

Edgerton, R.B. (1967) *The Cloak of Competence*. University of California Press, Berkeley.

——(1979) *Mental Retardation*. Fontana, London.

Evans, G., Todd, S., and Blunden, R. (1984) *Working in a Comprehensive*

Community-Based Service for Mentally Handicapped People: Research Report No. 16. Mental Handicap in Wales: Applied Research Unit, Cardiff.

Evans, G., Todd, S., Blunden, R., Porterfield, J., and Ager, A. (1987) 'Evaluating the Impact of a Move to Ordinary Housing', *British Journal of Mental Subnormality*, 33, 10-18.

Feinmann, M. (1987) 'The Development of Work Options for People with Severe Mental Handicap', In preparation.

Ferlie, E., Pahl, J., and Quine, L. (1984) 'Professional Collaboration in Services for Mentally Handicapped People', *Journal of Social Policy*, 13, 2.

Finch, J. (1984) 'Community Care: Developing Non-sexist Alternatives', *Critical Social Policy*, 9, Spring, 6-18.

Finch, J. and Groves, D. (1983) *A Labour of Love: Women, Work and Caring.* Routledge & Kegan Paul, London.

Firth, H. (1986) 'The Effectiveness of Parent Workshops in a Mental Handicap Service', *Child Care, Health and Development*, 8, 77-91.

Flynn, R.J. and Nitsch, K.E. (eds) (1980) *Normalization, Social Integration and Community Services.* University Park Press, Baltimore.

Frank, J.D. (1959) 'The Dynamics of the Therapeutic Relationship', *Psychiatry*, 22, 17-34.

Freedman, D. (1985) 'Rights and the Mentally Handicapped: An Effective Strategy', unpublished paper.

Freidson, E. (1970) *The Profession of Medicine.* Dodd, Mead & Co. Inc, New York.

Froland, C., Chapman, N.J., and Kiboko, P.J. (1981) *Helping Networks and Informal Services.* Sage, New York.

Gambrill, E.D. (1978) *Behaviour Modification: Handbook of Assessment, Interventions and Evaluations.* Jossey-Bass Inc., London.

Gardner, J. (1983) 'School-Based Parent Involvement: A Psychologist's View', in P. Mittler and H. McConachie (eds) *Parents, Professionals and Mentally Handicapped People.* Croom Helm, London.

Goffman, E. (1961) *Asylums: Essays on the Social Situation of Mental Patients and Other Inmates.* Penguin, Harmondsworth.

Gordon, R.A. (1980) 'Examining Labelling Theory: The Case of Mental Retardation', in W.R. Gove (ed.) *The Labelling of Deviance* (2nd edn). Sage, Beverley Hills.

Gove, W.R. (ed.) (1980) *The Labelling of Deviance.* (2nd edn). Sage, Beverley Hills.

Graham, H. (1984) *Women, Health and Family.* Wheatsheaf Books, London.

Gunzberg, H.C. (1975) 'Institutionalised People in the Community', *Research Exchange and Practice*, 1, 36-50.

Hallman, H.W. (1984) *Neighborhoods.* Sage, New York.

Harding, K., Baldwin, S., and Baser, C. (1986) 'Towards Multi-level Needs Assessments', *Behavioural Psychotherapy*, 15, 134-143.

Haug, M.R. and Sussman, M.B. (1969) 'Professional autonomy and the revolt of the client', *Social Problems*, 17, 153-161.

Henderson, P. and Thomas, D. (1980) *Skills in Neighbourhood Work.* Allen & Young, London.

Heron, A. and Myers, M. (1983) *Intellectual Impairment: The Battle Against*

Handicap. Academic Press, London.

HMSO (1913) *Mental Deficiency Act*. HMSO, London.

Horobin, G. (1983) 'Professional Mystery: The Maintenance of Charisma in General Medical Practice', in R. Dingwall and P. Lewis (eds) *The Sociology of the Professions*. Macmillan, London.

House of Commons Social Services Committee (1985) *Second Report 1984-85: Community Care*. HMSO, London.

Humphreys, S. and Blunden, R. (1987) 'A Collaborative Evaluation of an Individual Plan System', *British Journal of Mental Subnormality*, 23, 19-30.

Humphreys, S., Lowe, K., and Blunden, R. (1986) *Long-term Evaluation of Services for Mentally Handicapped People in Cardiff: Annual Report*. Mental Handicap in Wales, Applied Research Unit, Cardiff.

Humphreys, S., Lowe, K., and McLaughlin, S. (1985) *Long-term Evaluation of Services for Mentally Handicapped People in Cardiff: Consumer Satisfaction Report: 1984 Supplement*. Mental Handicap in Wales, Applied Research Unit, Cardiff.

Irvin, L.K., Crowell, F.A., and Bellamy, G.T. (1979) 'Multiple Assessment Evaluation of Programs for Severely Retarded Adults', *Mental Retardation*, 17, 123-128.

Jacques, E. (1989) *Requisite Organisation*, Cason Hall & Co. Gower, London.

Jay Committee (1979) *Report of the Committee of Inquiry into Mental Handicap Nursing and Care*, vol. 1. Cmnd. 7468-I, HMSO, London.

Keller, S. (1968) *The Urban Neighborhood: A Sociological Perspective*. Random House, New York.

Kendall, A. and Moss, P. (1972) *Integration or Segregation? The Future of Educational and Residential Services for Mentally Handicapped Children*. CMH, London.

Killilea, M. (1974) 'Mutual Help Organisations: Interpretations in the Literature', in G. Caplan (ed.) *Support Systems and Community Mental Health*. Basic Books, New York.

King, R.D., Raynes, N.V., and Tizard, J. (1971) *Pattern of Residential Services for Mentally Handicapped Children*. CMH, London.

King's Fund (1980) *An Ordinary Life: Comprehensive Locally Based Residential Services for Mentally Handicapped People*, King's Fund Project Paper No. 24. King's Fund Centre, London.

Korman, N. (1984) 'Paying for Community Care', *Health and Social Services Journal*, 12, 38-40.

Kratochwill, R.R. (1978) *Single Subject Research: Strategies for Evaluating Change*. Academic Press, New York.

Kurtz, R.A. (1975) 'Advocacy for the Mentally Retarded, The Development of a New Social Role', in M.J. Begab and S.A. Richardson (eds) *The Mentally Retarded and Society: A Social Science Perspective*. University Park Press, London.

Land, H. (1978) 'Who Cares for the Family?', *Journal of Social Policy*, 7, 357-384.

Lane, D., Noble, S., Tidball, M., and Twigg, S. (eds) (1983) *The Quiet Revolution*. Macmillan, London.

Leck, I., Gordon, W.L., and McKeown, T. (1967) 'Medical and Social Needs of

Patients in Hospitals for the Mentally Subnormal', *British Journal of Preventative and Social Medicine*, 21, 115-121.

Le Poidevin, S. (1985) 'Is there more in Portage than Education?', in B. Daly, J. Addington, S. Kerfoot, and S. Sigston (eds) (1985) *Portage: The Importance of Parents*. Nelson, Windsor.

Loney, M. (1981) 'The Politics of Self-help and Community Care', in A. Brechin, P. Liddard, and J. Swain (eds) *Handicap in a Social World*. Hodder & Stoughton, London.

Lopata, H.Z. (1976) 'Expertisation of Everyone and the Revolt of the Client', *Sociological Quarterly*, 17, 435-477.

Lynd, R.S. and Lynd, H.M. (1972) *Middletown: A Study in Contemporary American Culture*. Constable, New York.

McClaughry, J. (1980) 'Neighborhood Revitalization', in P. Duighnan and A. Ravushka (eds) *The United States in the 1980s*. Hoover Institution Press, Stanford.

McCloskey, H.J. (1980) 'Handicapped Persons and the Rights they Possess: The Right to Life, Liberty, Self-development and Development of Self', in R.S. Laura *The Problem of Handicap*. Macmillan, Melbourne.

McConachie, H. (1983a) 'Fathers, Mothers and Siblings: How Do They See Themselves?', in P. Mittler and H. McConachie (eds) *Parents, Professionals and Mentally Handicapped People*. Croom Helm, London.

——(1983b) 'Examples of Partnership in Europe', in P. Mittler and H. McConachie (eds) *Parents, Professionals and Mentally Handicapped People*. Croom Helm, London.

McConkey, R. and McCormack, B. (1983) *Breaking Barriers: Educating People about Disability*. Human Horizon Series, Cambridge.

Macdonald, I. (1981) 'Assessment a Social Dimension', in L. Barton and S. Tomlinson (eds) *Special Education Policy, Practices and Social Issues*. Harper & Row, London.

——(1984a) *Community Mental Handicap Teams*. Mental Handicap Services Unit Working Paper, BIOSS, London.

——(1984b) *Working Together: Professional Expectations and Understanding*. MHSU Working Paper, BIOSS, London.

Macdonald, I. and Couchman, T. (1978) *The Chart of Initiative and Independence*. NFER Nelson Publications, London.

Marks, L. (1980) *Parents' Needs and How to Meet Them: Modern Management of Mental Handicap*. MTP Press Ltd, London.

Mathey, A. and Vernick, J. (1975) 'Parents of Mentally Retarded Children: Emotionally Disturbed or Informationally Deprived?', in J.J. Dempsey (ed.) *Community Services for Retarded Children: The Consumer-provider Relationship*. University Park Press, Baltimore.

Mathieson, S. and Blunden, R. (1980) 'NIMROD is Piloting a Course Towards a Community Life', *Health and Social Services Journal*, 25 January, 122-124.

Mercer, J.R. (1973) *Labelling the Mentally Retarded: Clinical and Social System Perspectives on Mental Retardation*. University of California Press, Berkeley.

——(1975) 'Sociocultural Factors in Education Labelling', in M.J. Begab and

S.A. Richardson (eds) *The Mentally Retarded and Society: A Social Science Perspective*. University Park Press, London.

Mills, M.J. and Cummins, B.D. (1982) 'Deinstitutionalization Reconsidered', *International Journal of Law and Psychiatry*, 5, 271-284.

Mittler, P. (1977) Research to Practice in the Field of Handicap, *Journal of Practical Approaches to Developmental Handicap*, 1, 4–9.

——(1979) *People not Patients: Problems and Policies in Mental Handicap*. Methuen, London.

——(1983) 'Planning for Future Developments', in P. Mittler and H. McConachie (eds) *Parents, Professionals and Mentally Handicapped People*. Croom Helm, London.

Mittler, P. and McConachie, H. (1983a) 'Partnership and Parents: An Overview', in P. Mittler and H. McConachie (eds) *Parents, Professionals and Mentally Handicapped People*. Croom Helm, London.

——(1983b) (eds) *Parents, Professionals and Mentally Handicapped People*. Croom Helm, London.

Morris, P. (1969) *Put Away: A Sociological Study of Institutions for the Mentally Retarded*. Routledge & Kegan Paul, London.

Morris, T. and Morris, P. (1963) *Pentonville: A Sociological Study of an English Prison*. Routledge & Kegan Paul, London.

Murrell, S.A. and Norris, F.H. (1983) 'Quality of Life as the Criterion for Need Assessment and Community Psychology', *Journal of Community Psychology*, 11, 88-96.

National Council for Civil Liberties (1951) *50,000 Outside the Law*. NCCL, London.

Newson, E. (1981) 'Parents as a Resource in Diagnosis and Assessment', in A. Brechin, P. Liddiard, and J. Swain (eds) *Handicap in a Social World*. Hodder & Stoughton, Sevenoaks.

Nihira, K., Foster, R., Shellhaus, M. and Leland, H. (1975) *AAMD Adaptive Behaviour Scare for Children and Adults*. American Association for Mental Defiency, Washington. DC.

Nio Ong, B. (1983) 'Voluntary Organisation and Thatcher's Policies: An Overlap in Ideologies'. Paper presented at BSA Medical Sociology Conference, Sheffield.

Nirje, B. (1973) 'The Normalization Principle: Implications and Comments', in H.C. Gunzberg (ed.) *Advances in the Care of the Mentally Handicapped*. Bailliere Tindall, London.

Nissel, M. and Bonnerjea, L. (1982) *Family Care of the Handicapped Elderly: Who Pays?* Policy Studies Institute, London.

Oakley, A. (1974) *The Sociology of Housework*. Martin Robertson, Oxford.

O'Brien, J. (1974) 'Building Creative Tension: The Development of a Citizen Advocacy Programme for People with Mental Handicaps', in B. Sang and J. O'Brien *Advocacy: The UK and American Experience*, Kings Fund Project Paper No. 51. Kings Fund Centre, London.

O'Brien, J. and Tyne, A. (1981) *The Philosophy and Practice of Normalisation*. Campaign for the Mentally Handicapped, London.

O'Brien, J., Poole, C. and Galloway, C. (1981) *Accomplishments in Residential Services: Improving the Effectiveness of Residential Service Workers in*

Washington's Developmental Service System. Responsive Systems Associates, Atlanta, Georgia.

Oswin, M. (1971) *The Empty Hours: Allen Lane*. Penguin, London.

Owens, G. and Birchenall, P. (1979) *Mental Handicap: The Social Dimension*. Pitman, London.

Packwood, T. and Macdonald, I. (1978) 'The Organisation of Care for the Severely Mentally Handicapped', in E. Jaques (ed.) *Health Services*. Heinemann Educational Books, London.

Parham, J.D., Rude, C., and Bernanke, P. (1977) *Individual Program Planning and Developing Disabled Persons*. Research and Training Center in Medical Retardation, Texas Tech., Lubbock, Texas.

Plummer, K. (1979) 'Misunderstanding Labelling Perspectives', in D. Downes and P. Rock (eds) *Deviant Interpretations*. Martin Robertson, Oxford.

Porritt, J. (1984) *Seeing Green: The Politics of Ecology Explained*. Basil Blackwell Ltd, Oxford.

Praill, T. and Baldwin, S. (1986) 'Beyond Hero-Innovation: Real Change in Unreal Systems', *Behavioral Psychotherapy*, 16, 1-14.

Pugh, G. (1981) *Parents as Partners: Intervention Schemes and Group Work with Parents of Handicapped Children*. National Children's Bureau, London.

Pugh, G. and Russell, P. (1977) *Shared Care*. National Children's Bureau, London.

Repucci, N.D. (1977) 'Implementation Issues for the Behavior Modifier as Institutional Change Agent', *Behavior Therapy*, 8, 594-605.

Repucci, N.D., and Saunders, J.T. (1974) 'Social Psychology of Behavior Modifications: Problems of Implementation in Natural Settings', *American Psychologist*, 29, 649-660.

——(1979) 'History, Action and Change', *American Journal of Community Psychology*, 8.

Rescare (1985) *Resnews*, No. 4.

Richardson, A. (1984) *Working with Self-help Groups: A Guide for Local Professionals*. Bedford Square Press, London.

Richardson, A. and Goodman, M. (1983) *Self-help and Social Care: Mutual Aid for Modern Problems*. Policy Studies Institute, London.

Robinson, T. (1978) *In Worlds Apart: Professionals and their Clients in the Welfare State*. Bedford Square Press, London.

Roth, A.I. (1974) 'The Myth of Parental Attitudes', in D.M. Boswell and J.M. Winegrove (eds) *The Handicapped Person in the Community*. Tavistock, London.

Royal Commission (1957) *The Law Relating to Mental Illness and Mental Deficiency*. HMSO, London.

Russell, O. (1985) *Mental Handicap*. Churchill Livingston, London.

Ryan, J. and Thomas, F. (1980) *The Politics of Mental Handicap*. Penguin, Harmondsworth.

Sang, J.H. (1984) *Genetics and Development*. Longman, London.

——(1985) *Advocacy: The UK and USA Experience*. Kings Fund Project Paper No. 51. Kings Fund Centre, London.

Schur, E.M. (1971) *Labelling Deviant Behavior*. Harper & Row, New York.

Segal, S. (1984) *Society and Mental Handicap: Are We Educable?* Costello, Tunbridge Wells.

Simpkin, M. (1984) *Trapped Within Welfare; Surviving Social Work* (2nd edn). Macmillan, London.

Smith, J. (1984a) 'Stuck on the Transfer List', *Health and Social Services Journal*, 6, September.

——(1984b) 'Whose Turn to Carve the Joint?, *Health and Social Services Journal*, 13 October.

Social Services Committee (1985) The House of Commons, Second Report Sessions 1984-85 *Community Care with Special Reference to Adult Mentally Ill and Mentally Handicapped People*. HMSO, London.

Social Work Service Development Group (1984) *Supporting the Informal Carers: 'Fifty Styles of Caring'*. DHSS, London.

Stark, J.A., McGee, J.J., and Menolascino, F.J. (1985) *International Handbook of Community Services for the Mentally Retarded*. Lawrence Erlbaum Ass., Hillsdale, New Jersey.

Thomas, D., Firth, H., and Kendall, A. (1978) *ENCOR – A Way Ahead*. CMH, London.

Tizard, J. (1964) *Community Services for the Mentally Handicapped*. Oxford University Press, Oxford.

Tönnies, F. (1974) 'Gemeinschaft and Gelleschaft', in C. Bell and H. Newby (eds) *The Sociology of Community Care*.

Townsend, P. (1962) *The Last Refuge*. Routledge & Kegan Paul, London.

——(1969) 'Foreword: Social Planning for the Mentally Handicapped', in P. Morris, *Put Away: A Sociological Study of Institutions for the Mentally Retarded*. Routledge & Kegan Paul, London.

Turnbull, A. and Turnbull, H.R. (1982) 'Parent Involvement in the Education of Handicapped Children: A Critique', *Mental Retardation*, 20, 115-22.

Turnbull, A. and Winton, P.J. (1984) 'Parent Involvement, Policy and Practice: Current Research and Implications for Families of Young Severely Handicapped Children', in J. Blacher (ed.) *Severely Handicapped Children and their Families*. Academic Press, London.

Tyne, A. (1985) 'The New Apartheid', *Campaign for People with Mental Handicap: Newsletter*, 41, Summer, 2-3.

Vanier, J. (1976) in R. Kugel and A. Shearer (eds) *Changing Patterns of Residential Services for the Mentally Retarded*. President's Committee for the Mentally Retarded, Washington, DC.

——(1979) *Community and Growth*. Darton, Longman & Todd, London.

Ward, L. (1984) *Planning for People: Recruiting and Training Staff: Wells Road Project*, Kings Fund Project Paper No. 47, Kings Fund Centre, London.

Warnock Report (1978) *Special Education Needs: Report of the Committee of Inquiry into the Education of Handicapped Children and Young People*, Cmnd 7212. HMSO, London.

Warren, R.B. and Warren, D.I. (1977) *The Neighbourhood Organisers's Handbook*. University of Notre Dame Press, Notre Dame.

Welsh Office (1983) *All Wales Strategy for the Development of Services for Mentally Handicapped People*. Welsh Office, Cardiff.

West, H. (1985) 'The Sheer Jubilation she conveyed must be Meaningful in these Fractious and Depressing Times', *Guardian*, 19 December.

Whyte, W.F. (1955) *Street Corner Society: The Social Structure of an Italian Slum* (2nd edn), University of Chicago Press, Chicago.

Wilding, P. (1982) *Professional Power and Social Welfare*. Routledge & Kegan Paul, London.

Wilkin, D. (1977) *Family Care of the Severely Mentally Handicapped Child and the Decision to Seek Long-Term Institutional Care*. University of Manchester, Manchester.

——(1979) *Caring for the Mentally Handicapped Child*. Croom Helm, London.

Williams, P. and Shoultz, B. (1982) *We can speak for Ourselves: Self Advocacy by Mentally Handicapped People*. Human Horizons, Souvenir Press, London.

Wistow, G. (1983) 'Joint Finance in Community Care; have the incentives worked?', *Public Money*, 33-37.

Wolfensberger, W. (1969) 'The origin and nature of our institutional models', in W. Wolfensberger and R.B. Kugel (eds) (1969).

——(1972) *The Principle of Normalization in Human Services*. National Institute on Mental Retardation, Toronto.

——(1983) 'Social Role Valorization: A Proposed New Term for the Principle of Normalization', *Mental Retardation*, 21(6), 234-239.

Wolfensberger, W. and Glenn, S. (1973) *PASS 3: Program Analysis of Service Systems* (3rd edn). National Institute of Mental Retardation, Toronto.

Wolfensberger, W. and Kugel, R.B. (1969) (eds) *Changing Patterns in Residential Services for the Mentally Retarded*. Government Printing Office, Washington DC.

Worthington, A. (1984) *Coming to Terms with Mental Handicap*, Helena Press, London.

Wright, B.A. (1960) *Physical Disability: A Psychological Approach*. Harper & Row, New York.

Wright, K. and Haycox, A. (1984) *Public Sector Costs of Caring for Mentally Handicapped Persons in a Large Hospital*. University of York Centre for Health Economics, Discussion Paper No. 1, York.

Young, M.D. and Willmott, P. (1957) *Family and Kinship in East London*. Routledge & Kegan Paul, London.

Zastrow, C. (1983) 'Understanding and Preventing Burnout', *British Journal of Social Work*, April.

Name index

Name index

Flynn, R.J. 1
Frank, J.D. 79
Freedman, D. 132
Freidson, E. 74
Froland, C. 160

Gambrill, E.D. 5
Gardner, J. 77, 78
Glenn, S. 57
Goffman, E. 24, 51, 133
Goodman, M. 84
Gordon, R.A. 66
Gove, W.R. 66
Graham, H. 30
Groves, D. 102, 146, 152
Gunzberg, H.C. 64, 66

Hallman, H.W. 147, 151, 158, 162
Harding, K. 161, 165
Haycox, A. 104, 111, 112
Henderson, P. 147, 149, 151, 153, 155
Heron, A. 63, 64, 83
Horobin, G. 71
House of Commons Social Services Committee 125
Humphreys, S. 54, 58

Irvin, L.K. 57

Jacques, E. 140
Jay Committee 17–18, 22–3, 26, 27
Jeffree, D.J. 77

Keller, S. 146
Kendall, A. 17
Killilea, M. 84
King, R.D. 24, 25, 51
King's Fund 129, 132
Korman, N. 123
Kratochwill, R.R. 58
Kurtz, R.A. 85

Land, H. 30
Landesman-Dwyer, S. 52
Lane, D. 62, 63
Leck, I. 21
Le Poidevin, S. 71

Loney, M. 84
Lynd, H.M. 20
Lynd, R.S. 20

McClaughry, J. 147
McConachie, H. 69, 74, 75, 76
McConkey, R. 38
McCormack, B. 38
Macdonald, I. 128, 134, 138
Marks, L. 40
Mathey, A. 67, 73, 75
Mathieson, S. 54
Mercer, J.R. 14–16, 66
Mills, M.J. 145
Mittler, P. 38, 52, 63, 64, 66, 69, 70, 74, 75, 76, 77, 79, 80, 82
Morris, P. 16, 24–5
Morris, T. 24
Moss, P. 17
Murrell, S.A. 150, 165
Myers, M. 63, 64, 83

National Council for Civil Liberties 21
Newson, E. 75
Nihira, K. 59
Nio Ong, B. 4
Nirje, B. 1, 87
Nissel, M. 30
Nitsch, K.E. 1
Norris, F.H. 150, 165

Oakley, A. 29
O'Brien, J. 53, 64, 65, 67, 147
Oswin, M. 51
Owens, G. 72

Packwood, T. 128
Parham, J.D. 158
Plummer, K. 66
Porritt, J. 6, 8, 10
Praill, T. 155, 160
Pugh, G. 72, 74, 75, 76

Repucci, N.D. 52, 157
Rescare 82, 83
Richardson, A. 84
Robinson, T. 67, 71

Subject index

Adaptive Behaviour Scale (ABS) 59
advocacy: citizen 85–6, 159; self-84–5, 159
agencies: the assault on 23–8; vs. family care 22; and mental handicap 18; *see also* local authorities
All Wales Strategy for the Development of Services for Mentally Handicapped People 59–60
'apartheid' approach (Tyne) 64, 96, 98
L'Arche (France) 89–95
ascertainment 13; rates 21
assertiveness training 72

behavioural approach 5; dangers of 66; and normalisation 8
Brooklands Unit 26
budgeting for services 124–5, 162

Campaign for Mentally Handicapped People (CMH) 17
Camphill Villages 95
care in the community (UK) 4, 9, 27, 123–4; burden of 31–2; costs of 103–17; critique of 145–6; definition of 28; and feminism 28–33; vs. neighbourhood work 153, 160; shared 40; White Paper (1989) 126–7
child-care: gender roles in 30
children in care: Brooklands Unit 26;

treatment of 25–6, 51
clients: inhibition of 71–2; rights of 74
colony system, *see* mental deficiency colony
community: vs. neighbourhood 146; studies 19–20, 21, 23; team 38, 157–9; traditional 19, 20; *see also* care in the community, neighbourhoods
community care, *see* care in the community
cost–benefit analysis, 102, 156
counselling: and mental handicap 35–7 *passim*; 42

Danish Mental Retardation Act 1
data collection, *see* evaluation
Denmark: normalisation in 1–2
developmental theory 140–2
deviance 17; social-reaction model 13–14, 18
domestic labour: division of 29–31
Down's syndrome 46, 78; informing parents of 36–7

Eastern Nebraska Community Office of Retardation (ENCOR) 17
ecological perspective 6–11 *passim*
economics of service provision 100–28, 162; agency services 124–5; 'care in the community' 123–4; costs of care 103–17; economic appraisal 101–3;

180